Development policies:
sociological perspectives

Development policies: sociological perspectives

Edited by
Anthony Hall *and* James Midgley

Manchester University Press
Manchester and New York
Distributed exclusively in the U.S.A. and Canada
by **St. Martin's Press**, New York

Published by Manchester University Press
Oxford Road, Manchester M13 9PL

Distributed exclusively in the USA and Canada
by St. Martin's Press Inc.,
175 Fifth Avenue, New York 10010, USA

British Library cataloguing in publication data
Hall, Anthony
   Development policies: sociological
   perspectives.
   1. Economic development –
   Social aspects
   I. Title   II. Midgley, James
   306'.3   HD75

Library of Congress cataloging in publication data
Development policies.
   Bibliography: p. 134.
   Includes index.
   1. Economic development—Social aspects.
2. Developing countries—Social policy. 3. Developing
countries—Economic policy. I. Hall, Anthony L.,
1947–   . II. Midgley, James.
HD75.D49   1988   303.4'4   87-31462
ISBN 0-7190-2274-6

Phototypeset in Linotron Plantin
by Northern Phototypesetting Co., Bolton
Printed and bound in Great Britain by
Anchor Brendon Ltd, Tiptree, Essex

Contents

Introduction   *Anthony Hall and James Midgley*

During recent decades, after centuries of European imperial rule, struggles for national independence in Africa, Asia and parts of Central and South America have resulted in a major restructuring of the old world order. New nation states, no longer administered directly through local colonial bureaucracies from the capital cities of Europe, emerged within the official boundaries created by imperialism. Previously suppressed nationalist movements took control of the institutions of power and abolished the structures of racial exclusivity and privilege that characterised colonial society. These events were of enormous political and historical significance, and it is not surprising that they attracted widespread attention from academic social scientists in the West who had previously been parochially limited by their national experiences when explaining social reality. Economists, political scientists, historians, geographers, sociologists and others began to ask questions of analytical significance about the changes that were taking place. Specialisms emerged within these disciplines to speculate on these developments and gradually, as different social scientists began to collaborate with each other, interdisciplinary insights into the developing societies and their dynamics emerged.

Analytical inquiry into the developing societies has been accompanied by normative speculation about the processes that might transform the predominantly agrarian economies of the colonised world into economically self-sufficient industrial societies. It was generally assumed that social science knowledge gleaned from a proper understanding of these processes could be applied to assist the governments of the newly emergent states to plan the modernisation of their economies and the transformation of their social structures. Through

planning and administration, measures could be adopted that would
eradicate the causes of backwardness and dependency. The term
development has been widely employed to denote this activity and, in
addition to comprising a practical enterprise undertaken by
governmental organisations, international agencies, voluntary bodies
and commercial enterprises, it has engaged the resources of academic
social scientists. It has involved analytical speculation about the conditions of underdevelopment as well as normative theories concerning
the best way of promoting economic and social progress. Indeed, the
study of development is explicitly normative, invoking evaluative
criteria, ideologies and moral judgements. It is also an applied field of
academic endeavour concerning itself with technical methodologies
for promoting economic and social progress in the developing societies. Professional training for development planners, administrators
and researchers is now offered at various institutions of higher learning in both the industrial and developing countries.

As an academic activity, development has been most vigorously and
successfully pursued by economists who now dominate the field.
They are also primarily responsible for the articulation of general
theories of development and for the formulation of policy prescriptions which govern the developmental activities of public agencies in
many countries. Economists are also primarily responsible for the
implementation of development strategies. Together with planners
and administrators, they manage the policy-making organisations, in
both national and international contexts that advocate the ideals of
modernisation, change and growth. The declared intention of the
governments of the newly independent states to transform their
subsistence economies offered useful opportunities for the application
of economic knowledge to the problems of underdevelopment. By
providing policy prescriptions for rapid growth based on plausible
explanations of the causes of backwardness, economists greatly
enhanced their stature and gained a virtual monopoly of the field.
Their accounts of the nature of underdevelopment have been widely
accepted by political elites in the developing societies, aid officials in
the industrial nations and international civil servants. They have also
structured the way other social scientists have approached development questions. In their efforts to contribute to the formulation of
useful policy measures, political scientists, public administrators,
geographers and others generally accepted the imperative of economic
change and a vision of progress governed by economic ideals.

Although some sociologists have been interested in development questions and in the formulation of policies designed to promote the economic and social transformation of Third World societies, this is not a well developed specialism within the discipline. Although sociologists have helped to construct conceptual approaches to the analysis of development phenomena, and have enriched the interdisciplinary paradigms which had emerged to organise research in the field, they have been unduly dependent on economic conceptions. Also, sociological inquiry into development has been primarily concerned with theoretical speculation rather than the identification of policy prescriptions and their involvement in the identification and evaluation of development policy has been limited. While sociologists do find employment in development settings, their involvement has been limited. Compared to the deployment of economists and administrative scientists, there are relatively few opportunities for the practical engagement of sociologists in development planning and sociologists are not prominent either in development policy organisations in the developing societies or in the international agencies. This is true also of development aid organisations where it is now more widely recognised that a broader multidisciplinary approach that combines technical, economic, political, material and human considerations is required. Although many aid organisations recognise that a sociological input is worthwhile, sociologists are still usually employed as temporary consultants to comment on the social implications of particular programmes. Even in the enlightened 1980s, when development thinking has been dominated by poverty oriented and 'basic needs' approaches, sociologists have not participated in development policy-making organisations on an equal footing with economists and public administrators.

There are several reasons for this state of affairs. In some cases, the under-utilisation of sociologists is due to ignorance about the sociologist's technical abilities and potential value, and in some cases it is because of a mistaken belief that sociologists are purveyors of left-wing ideologies. Indeed, the term 'sociology' is often confused with socialism. This attitude has been particularly common among technical personnel and it is not surprising that sociologists have not always been welcomed in development organisations nor accepted as useful members on development project teams. Although it is now quite common for aid agencies to require sociological involvement in development projects, aid administrators often bypass official concern for a sociological perspective on development policy. But sociologists are also responsible for their lack of involvement in the field of development policy. The lack of a body of normative theory that can guide sociological praxis, and the disdain for practical matters within the discipline have discouraged extensive sociological involvement in development. Unlike economists, who have a clearly formulated job description based on their academic training, sociologists must pioneer their own roles in development settings. In the absence of a coherent conception of their task, it is hardly surprising that the aid agencies and other development organisations are ill-informed about the potential value of the sociologist's contribution.

Although sociological involvement in development is limited and based on a poorly formulated notion of practical engagement, this book argues that sociologists do have an important role to play in the formulation, implementation and assessment of development policies. The various authors reveal that sociologists can contribute to the development policy process and foster a broader appreciation of the social dimensions of development. Sociologists have expertise in providing social information for development policy-making, assisting in the determination of the social objectives of plans, broadening the criteria that are used when formulating proposals, understanding the human failings of implementation, evaluating the impact of programmes and measuring the wider social effects of purposeful intervention. Because of their training, sociologists are particularly sensitive to those intangible social realities which defy quantification and objectification. They are also particularly concerned with the neglected aspects of development such as culture, the status of women and the subjective human experience of poverty and deprivation.

This is not to suggest that sociological involvement in development policy offers new, magical solutions to the complex and often apparently intractable problems facing policy-makers. Today there is a tendency to assume that a proper sociological input will provide solutions where other approaches have failed. In fact, the increasing involvement of sociologists in aid projects has been prompted by a high rate of project failure. Although sociologists are being called upon more frequently to diagnose what had gone wrong and to devise appropriate solutions, it is fallacious to conclude that they have an instant formula for success. This is a simplistic view, which is not conducive to the adoption of a broadly-based interdisciplinary approach in which sociological knowledge is applied together with the insights of other disciplines and the expertise of practitioners to provide a balanced, reasoned and appropriate approach to policy problems.

While this book is committed to the idea that sociologists have an important contribution to make to development policy, it recognises that their involvement raises a number of difficult issues. Indeed, the very concept of development, with its Western connotations of progress through rational planning, its Utopian and humanitarian values and its faith in the promise of science, is complex and contentious. Given the institutionalisation of these assumptions of development thinking, sociologists have legitimately asked whether engagement in development policy and the acceptance of its values is desirable. Indeed, sociologists have long been ambivalent about policy involvement in general. The conventional view, which has been propounded since the nineteenth century, is that sociology's objectivity and the discipline's analytical sophistication will inevitably suffer through the attempts of sociologists to organise society. Although many sociologists have questioned this argument, suggesting that ethical neutrality is an unattainable ideal, many recognise at the same time that ethical presumption impedes the attainment of analytical clarity.

With the radicalisation of Western sociology in the 1960s and 1970s, a different version of the policy involvement issue gained currency in academic circles. Reduced to its crudest tenets, this argument held that meaningful opportunities for policy intervention could be found only in the revolutionary transformation of society. Attempts to apply sociological knowledge in any other context were condemned as being likely to result in no more than token reforms. Some exponents of this view extended the argument to suggest that development policy in the Third World was conspiratorially suppressive of popular discontent and that sociologists who engaged in policy related activities were providing tacit support for oppressive political systems. The popularity of these views was hardly conducive to fostering academic interest in policy issues and unwittingly reinforced the discipline's conventional conservative belief in ethical neutrality.

Although it is a legitimate point of view, the radical academic critique of development policy involvement has been clouded by a vulgarisation of Marxian ideas and is open to a charge of irrelevance to the real problems of the modern world. The teaching that Utopia can be found only in revolution is not only silly but fails to provide a rationale for those who wish to express their commitment to progressive change through engagement in the development field. Also, it may be argued that academic sociologists owe it to their students to provide guidelines for those who study the subject with a view to pursuing a career related to their education. This is particularly important in view of the fact that sizeable numbers of students study sociology with the hope of finding employment in governmental organisations concerned with development policy. It is not much use to them to learn that a morally acceptable career in development sociology is to be found in the pursuit of revolutionary action.

This is not to reject the importance of maintaining a critical stance on development policy issues. Indeed, sociology's potent techniques of analysis have much to contribute to the constructive assessment of policy. Sociologists may critically examine policies without tainting their integrity, sacrificing analytical objectivity or being supportive of evil regimes. They can also contribute positively to the promotion of socially just forms of policy intervention and assist in the formation of acceptable ethical criteria for involvement. The pessimism of much radical sociological writing on development is not conducive to the very ideals that many radical sociologists hold dear.

These and other arguments about sociological involvement in development policy reveal that the issue is problematic and that many questions arising out of the involvement of sociologists in the field are difficult to answer. Should sociologists seek to analyse development from an independent, critical, vantage point or should they work in development planning organisations attempting to influence policy directly? What ethical criteria should govern sociological involvement in development activities? To what extent can sociologists divorce wider political and ideological considerations from specific technical tasks and thus claim to be guided purely by expertise and not by values? Sociologists need to debate issues of sociological engagement in development much more thoroughly if they are to answer these and other questions. They need also to present a coherent case for the adoption of a sociological perspective in development activities and they need to show in concrete terms how sociological involvement in the development policy-making process can bring beneficial results. While this task is substantial and cannot be dealt with fully in this volume, some aspects of sociological involvement in development policy are discussed in the following chapters.

The first chapter by James Midgley, which is intended to serve as a broad introduction to the book, surveys the issues arising from the involvement of academic and professional sociologists in development policy-making, planning and administration in developing societies. Tracing the emergence of development as a policy enterprise, the author shows that the subject has been sadly neglected by sociologists. The chapter makes a strong case for the more systematic and explicit involvement of sociologists in development policy, arguing that sociological engagement in the field is urgently needed in view of the essentially social nature of the development process. In addition, sociology needs to address policy issues directly since there is an increasing demand for professional sociologists in the field. Although Midgley recognises that sociological involvement raises difficult ethical and professional problems, these need to be dealt with and not avoided. A stance of non-involvement does little to meet the needs of professional sociologists who are regularly being called on to serve in policy-making capacities in organisations concerned with development. At present they lack clear normative approaches on which to base their professional roles. Reviewing some of the tasks sociologists in development agencies presently undertake, and considering the relevance of the discipline's academic content on development questions, he explores some of the issues related to sociology's contribution to the development task.

In the second chapter, Anthony Hall examines the role of sociologists in the planning and implementation of foreign aid-funded development projects, drawing particular attention to the relative dearth of sociological involvement in the field. Hall's account, which is one of the first of its kind, examines the major academic, technocratic, institutional and political reasons for this situation and concludes that a major difficulty is the tendency of sociologists to adopt a critical stance towards official wisdom. Unlike many other professionals engaged in the aid industry, such as economists and engineers, sociologists are liable to challenge conventional approaches and this does not make them popular in official aid circles. While sociologists are finding more frequent employment opportunities in aid programmes, their limited role as advisers on the 'social aspects' of aid projects hinders their ability to make a significant contribution; they will only begin to make a major impact when they are able to acquire decision-making power within the aid bureaucracies themselves.

Chapter 3 by Martin Bulmer reviews the contribution of sociological research to the formulation and implementation of development policy. This is one field in which sociologists have a unique and significant role to play. Reviewing the use of social surveys, ethnographic studies, secondary analysis of census and other data, the construction of social indicators, and evaluation research, Bulmer shows that sociologists can provide extremely useful factual information for policy-making. Drawing examples from the fields of population, health and social security policy, he highlights the problems of collecting high quality data in the development context and suggests ways of improving the data collection process. He also pays attention to the ethical and political dimensions of research into the process by which development policy is formulated and promulgated.

The next chapter, by Margaret Hardiman, uses the insights of sociology to examine the impact of development policies on the position of women in developing societies. This is a neglected issue which is amenable to sociologicial analysis and has indeed, been brought to the attention of policy-makers largely through the efforts of sociologists. Hardiman discusses the impact of development policies on women and reveals the erroneous assumptions frequently made by policy-makers about womens' roles. Since the policy-makers are invariably men, development policies often reflect a one-sided male perspective, resulting in the adoption of measures that ignore the needs of one half of the population. The male-dominated view of development needs to be corrected by the provision of sociological data which give a more accurate perspective on women in the development context. Reviewing policies and programmes that have been sensitive to the needs of women, Hardiman shows how the position of women in developing societies can be improved and considers some of the lessons that can be learned.

In Chapter 5, Anthony Hall explores the nature of popular participation in the field of rural development and seeks to show how a sociological perspective can be usefully applied to clarify the parameters, limitations and potential applicability of this concept. It examines the growing popularity among policy-makers of the concept of popular participation and focuses on the constraints inherent in State-directed forms of participation by referring to case study material from China, Ethiopia, India and Tanzania. The role of non-government agencies is also examined and, although these organisations offer more scope for encouraging authentic forms of people's involvement, serious obstacles remain. Hall argues that a sociological analysis of the concept of popular participation is particularly useful since it highlights not only certain conceptual shortcomings which are often overlooked but also fundamental limitations in attempting to put such notions into practice.

In the final chapter Norman Long examines the role of the State in agrarian development, from a distinctly sociological perspective. He considers three major contrasting analytical approaches (structural analysis, the institution–incorporation model and the actor-oriented approach) and considers the contribution of each to clarifying the logic of agrarian change. Long concludes that, while all three contribute in their own ways to our understanding of development policy-making and implementation, none on its own offers a completely satisfactory explanation. He suggests combining elements of all three in an 'interface' analysis which would facilitate comprehension of the interaction between local circumstances and State policy formulation, in areas such as State–peasant relations for example, within the broader structural framework of agrarian change.

There are many other topics related to sociological involvement in development policy which cannot be included here. It is not only a question of limitations of space but a consequence of the enormity of the field, indeed, it is doubtful whether such a broad topic can be exhausted in one volume, however sizeable. Nevertheless, the material presented here should be sufficiently wide-ranging to provide a useful introduction to a neglected field. It is also hoped that the book will encourage sociologists to consider the issues raised more thoroughly, and that a more widespread discussion of their role in development will ensue. We would like to think that economists and other social scientists, as well as planners and administrators, will also find it useful. Since few decision-makers in the developing societies have an adequate appreciation of sociology's distinctive disciplinary character and professional potential, it is hoped that the topics discussed may illuminate and inform and demonstrate the value of a broadly-based sociological contribution to development policy.

1 James Midgley

Sociology and development policy

In its quest to facilitate the production of knowledge about the social world, sociology conforms to the canons of scholarly inquiry. Like the other social sciences, it has institutionalised the rules of scientific investigation to study social phenomena; deductive logic, empiricism and verification through experimental design are characteristics of its methodology that are widely, albeit variously, used. Sociology began to achieve recognition as an academic discipline towards the end of the nineteenth century when the first courses in the subject were introduced at European and North-American universities. Much sociology is, of course, social philosophy and as such the discipline's antecedents may be traced back to the ancients. But the application of positivist methodology to the study of social phenomena and the incorporation of sociology within the academic community was only achieved during the late nineteenth century. As the result of the incremental accretion of descriptive studies, statistical reports, speculative treatises and other types of investigation that conformed to the new scientific ethos of the time, sociological writings attracted attention and gained respectability. These pioneering efforts formed the constituent elements of sociology's emerging corpus of knowledge on which its disciplinary formalisation would be based.

Although paralleled by the other emerging social sciences, and the rapid expansion of knowledge in general, sociology's achievements over the last hundred years have been significant. Formative courses in the subject have been constituted into autonomous academic departments which have proliferated rapidly with the result that few universities in the Western world are now without them. Today, a plethora of journals, books, research reports, professional associations, and conferences attest to the subject's maturity. Few would deny that sociology has facilitated the production of knowledge about the social world on a grand scale. A vast amount of factual information about human populations, social stratification, family functioning, social problems, the dynamics of social change, the properties of organisations and a great variety of other social phenomena is now available.

Flattering commentaries about the undoubted achievements of sociology must, however, be tempered by the realisation that numerous methodological and other problems still impede the discipline's development. Many of these are, of course, common to the other social sciences as well but, in some cases, they are particularly marked within the realm of sociological investigation. Sociology suffers from a proclivity for vagueness. Although the problem also occurs in economics and psychology, it is more marked in sociology. Social realities are difficult to define, let alone measure, and it is not surprising that the concepts, terminologies and operational definitions sociologists employ suffer from a lack of standardisation. Concepts are often loosely formulated and usually remain vague because attempts to define them precisely frequently degenerate into semantic squabbles. Unlike the natural sciences, sociology is disadvantaged by the absence of a stable, unitary paradigmatic conception of the social universe within which routine science can be practised. Competing schema are used to frame both speculative and empirical inquiry and, in addition to fostering the fragmentation of the subject, the prevalence of different approaches is also conducive to faddishness; it has also produced a situation where painstaking empirical research undertaken within the framework of one conceptual system is rendered obsolete by the demise of its popularity.

Another problem facing contemporary sociology concerns the span of its subject matter. Its scope is exceedingly broad and frequently sociological research overlaps the boundaries of the other social sciences. In some cases, such as that of social anthropology, the demarcation of disciplinary territory is particularly hard to establish. Disagreements about the proper unit for sociological analysis also hamper disciplinary integrity. While some argue that sociological investigation should focus on the patterns of interaction that take place at the micro level of inter-personal encounters, others believe that the discipline should concern itself with the study of societies (which are usually operationalised as nation states). Some sociologists even argue that the discipline's unit of analysis should be the world social system as a whole. These very different views on sociology's proper scope hamper the production of a common core of knowledge which sociologists can claim as their own.

A problem which is of particular relevance to this book concerns the discipline's ambivalence on the question of the application of sociological knowledge to policy. The distinction between 'basic' and 'applied' sociology does not exist in any meaningful sense and, in spite of a long-standing debate on the issue, sociologists remain divided as to whether they should seek to apply knowledge to modify social realities or whether they should remain detached from the world of practical concerns. While some argue that sociology's quest for pure knowledge will be impeded by the deliberate production of policy-relevant research, others take the view that all sociological inquiry is rooted in values and preconceptions and that attempts to attain ethical neutrality are futile. Others point to the enormity of social illfare in modern times arguing that it is morally indefensible to adopt a non-interventionist stance when human suffering is all pervasive and when sociological technology has meliorative relevance.

The question of policy engagement is particularly apposite in the context of Third World development where the poverty and deprivation experienced by hundreds of millions of people calls for the application of workable remedies based on scientifically tested knowledge. The essentially social character of the condition of underdevelopment would appear also to be highly conducive to policies and programmes which employ sociological expertise. But the sociological literature on the subject seldom addresses these issues in terms that have direct policy significance. Although sociological research into the developing societies, their peoples, cultures and institutions has been extensive, sociologists have made a comparatively small contribution to development as a policy process. In spite of its potential for engagement in the field and the need for sociological insights, sociology remains peripheral to the development task. It is time that sociologists considered the matter properly and began to debate the desirability and implications of policy involvement in the field. To ignore the issue is not only morally questionable but, in view of the significance of development in our time, is a gross oversight.

The enterprise of development

'Development' and its various synonyms and euphemisms has

become a commonplace word which everybody uses and apparently understands. But in academic circles where popular terms are often defined differently and with a greater measure of scepticism, the concept remains elusive. There are formidable terminological difficulties in using the word and the term is also open to a variety of interpretations. Development has been conceptualised as a process of economic growth fostered by industrial investment and a competitive culture of enterprise and profit maximisation. It has been defined as liberation from the strictures of colonial and imperial domination in which nations secure the right to self-determination and self-reliance. It has also been viewed as a state of welfare in which ordinary people enjoy freedom from want, disease, ignorance, insecurity, exploitation and oppression.

Although only popularised in recent times, the concept of development is not a new one. Contemporary development ideals are deeply rooted in Western culture, appearing in seminal form in early Utopian tracts and discourses on the idea of progress. In the nineteenth century, a matured version of the notion of progress fused with evolutionary concepts in biology to produce social theories which justified European 'superiority' and imperial domination and, at the same time, offered the prospect of progress to societies that were then regarded as primitive. Colonialism gave tangible expression to these ideas by simultaneously exploiting and modernising. The construction of railways and other transport and communications networks, the introduction of an administrative system which maintained law and order and created stability for orderly investment, and the establishment of plantations, mines and processing industries were early forms of development effort that enriched the imperial powers but also laid the foundations for the subsequent modernisation of production in many colonised territories. The dual mandate may have been reprehensible but, as Marx realised, imperial penetration of the pre-capitalist societies created a dynamic of ineluctable change (Melotti 1977).

The precursors of modern-day development policies also emerged during the colonial period. Ghana is reputed to have been the setting for the first of several colonial development plans which, on a piecemeal basis, sought to co-ordinate public sector investment primarily in infrastructure to aid economic growth (Waterston 1965). The concept of colonial development, which was enshrined in the British *Colonial Development Act* of 1929, was another major step in the emergence of development policy. Although intended to promote the export of manufactured goods to the colonies and thus to stimulate domestic industry, it legitimated large-scale interventionism in a prevailing climate of *laissez-faire* and accelerated the adoption of planning on a more comprehensive scale. These formative efforts were later combined with the notion of centrally-directed economic growth derived from the Soviet experience of planning to establish an all-embracing conception of integrated economic, social and physical development which would orchestrate the modernisation of the newly independent societies. The achievement of sovereignty by nationalist movements put these ideals into effect in a systematic way. Central organisations concerned with development planning were established to concretise the notion of development and to translate it into policy terms. Development ceased to be the summation of the activities of a myriad of producers or an abstract theoretical ideal and instead became the managed implementation of purposeful policies. Operationalised through public and private investments in productive enterprises and infrastructural projects, and measured in terms of GNP growth, development became a policy science.

As a policy science, development drew extensively on the concepts and theories of the Western social sciences and on institutionalised cultural beliefs in progress, technology and growth. Of most immediate significance was the work of economists who drew on earlier attempts at colonial development, the experience of industrialisation in Europe, and Keynsian and other forms of economic planning to offer models for the transformation of the economies of the newly emergent nations that were both analytical and normative in character. Analytical accounts pointed to the existence of a dualistic economy characterised by a large backward traditional sector (which supported the bulk of the population in subsistence poverty) and a small modern sector which had been introduced during the colonial period (Boeke 1953; Higgins 1956). Normative prescriptions proposed solutions based on policies that would promote rapid industrialisation, stimulate growth, absorb surplus labour and deplete the subsistence economy (United Nations 1951; Lewis 1954). As the economic history of the West and studies of the development of Southern and Eastern Europe by Rosenstein-Rodan (1943) had revealed, industrialisation held the key to progress. Industrialisation increased the productive capacity of the economy beyond the imagination of the agrarian producer, mobilised labour on a vast scale, introduced wage incomes, created a demand for goods and services and set into a motion a spiral of growth that would eventually abolish mass poverty.

The interventionist values embodied in these normative theories contrasted sharply with the prevailing ideology of liberalism in Western social science. In spite of the impact of these ideas in policy circles, planning was regarded by most academic economists and other social scientists at the time as an unwarranted and potentially harmful practice which would stifle entrepreneurship and retard the inherent dynamic of the capitalist system. Some such as Hayek (1944) took the view that planning was little more than a technology of totalitarianism which, by seeking to regulate social and economic life, was essentially oppressive. However, many accepted the argument that planning could be useful in the context of underdevelopment, serving as a means for stimulating economic growth and directing the process of orderly change. But it was regarded as a short-term measure. When planning had fulfilled its role as the initiator of economic change, the profit motive rather than centralised direction should guide the subsequent modernisation of Third World societies.

The disdain for planning in Western social science was not, however, translated into official policy in the developing societies. Far from abandoning the notion of interventionism, the nationalist and populist leaders of the newly independent states embraced it. Indeed, they soon transcended the limited interventionist ideals inherent in the original conception of economic planning to foster a more general commitment to statism and centralism which expanded rapidly into all spheres of economic and social life. Facilitated by various motives, the interventionist ideologies of the emergent states facilitated the rapid expansion of the public sector. The international agencies, and the United Nations in particular, encouraged this trend by actively promoting the creation of centralised planning agencies and support- ing the expansion of state-managed productive enterprises, public education, health and other social services and similar governmental activities. Paradoxically, the Western powers also endorsed the inter- ventionist tendency in the Third World. The Americans recognised that the Marshall Plan had made a dramatic contribution to the reconstruction of the axis economies and, as the Cold War intensified, the need to find an antidote to the appeal of Communism became a pressing concern. Since it was believed that planning could raise the levels of living of those who were most susceptible to the lure of subversion, the promotion of development became a foreign policy objective.

Transcending earlier conceptions of planning as an instrument for the acceleration of economic growth, the concept of development now emerged to institutionalise the idea of widespread State intervention directed at the improvement of social and economic conditions and the promotion of the comprehensive modernisation of the developing societies. By the 1960s, when the United Nations declared the first 'Development Decade', development had become a major enterprise. Drawing on the wisdom of the social sciences, the passion of interventionist ideologies, the aspirations of nationalists and the promise of modern science and technology, development has been pursued by a great variety of governmental bodies in many different countries, by large international development agencies, by voluntary organisations and commerical firms, by research institutions and universities and by hundreds of millions of ordinary people in the developing societies who, singularly or in association with each other, seek to improve the quality of their lives.

The common values of development have, however, been questioned in recent years. The realities of world recession, superpower struggles for global dominance, civil conflicts, famines and persistent poverty have dampened the optimistic assumptions that underly original development ideals. As the brutality of dictatorship, the pervasiveness of institutionalised corruption and the burden of overstaffed bureaucracies in many developing societies have been recognised, the Western social democratic notion of the State as the purveyor of the common good has been also shaken. This is equally true of the once unquestioned acceptance of the benefits of Western scientific invention, and scepticism about the virtues of relentless technological innovation has increased. The formative conception of development as modernisation through the promotion of domestic industrialisation has also been questioned as competing paradigms have emerged in academic development circles. These conflicting schema have fragmented the study of development and hampered the adoption of a unitary set of policies and programmes that can be implemented and evaluated. Growing controversies about the meaning of development have also caused a good deal of confusion in the field. The previously accepted tenets of development have been challenged, creating a diversity of opinions which have not been resolved.

However, these difficulties have not deflected from the declared commitment to planned and technologically propelled development by many Third World governments. In spite of the problems associated with its use, the notion of development continues to have an essential reality, finding tangible expression in the policies and programmes of contemporary States throughout the modern world. Furthermore, although dominated by economists, development as a policy task is amenable to the application of sociological insights.

Sociology and the neglect of development

Sociology has long been interested in questions which have relevance to the study of development. One of these, which was a major concern in the discipline's formative years, is the issue of how societies experience change and are transformed from small, simple structures into large, complex systems. Nineteenth-century sociologists offered different answers to this question and, as a part of this speculative enterprise, they produced a variety of typological schema that categorised the process of development into a number of discrete stages. In their accounts, societies were conceived as developing along a linear, progressive path, passing through successive stages, each of which is characterised by particular forms of social organisation.

Although essentially analytical in their intent, sociological theories of societal change have normative implications. This is explicit in the work of Comte and Marx but also in accounts where prescriptive notions find expression in the idea that technological invention and social progress will improve society. Another normative dimension of these theories which generated concern in the early decades of this century, and particularly in American sociological circles, was the belief that change was a negative dynamic that facilitated the disruption of social life, weakened cherished institutions and increased the incidence of social pathology. Drawing inspiration from conservative and predominantly agrarian elements within the American sociological establishment, the conceptualisation of social changes as the source of social pathology challenged previously established progressivist beliefs and gave impetus to the idea that sociological knowledge should be applied to minimise its destructive consequences.

This idea found expression in the concept of social planning which, it appears, was first given currency in the 1930s (Midgley 1984a). Drawing on the work of Ogburn, the notion of social planning was explicitly normative, claiming that sociological knowledge could be applied through legislation, education, propaganda and leadership to limit the harmful effects of social change such as crime, alchoholism, falling moral standards, family disorganisation and other 'social pathologies' of the time. Social planning could also seek to direct the process of change ensuring that it would propel society towards predetermined desirable goals, strengthen the social fabric and enhance social functioning. But the sociological literature on social planning remained vague about the procedures and techniques that sociologists could employ in their attempts to manage the effects of change. Apart from condemnatory observations on the evils of social pathology and moral exhortations for social betterment, few tangible prescriptions were provided.

Although the study of social change and the concept of social planning have direct significance for the study of Third World development, and could have formed the basis for the formulation of a coherent and distinctly sociological approach to the subject, sociology's contribution to the field has been limited. While deeply rooted in sociology's history, the idea of social planning was not generally commended. The study of social change was also relegated. With the rise of functionalist sociology, the belief in the 'natural' workings of the social system and in its inherent tendency towards stability, consensus and re-equilibration gained widespread support. This view of social reality weakened the discipline's formative interests in social change and the topic was increasingly neglected.

The demise of social change as a primary sociological concern and the abandonment of the interventionist principles contained in sociological accounts of social planning, impeded sociology's potential for becoming involved in development in a meaningful way. In spite of the discipline's long-standing interest in the subject, relatively few sociologists embraced the study of Third World development when this field of academic endeavour began to emerge as a distinctive specialism in the 1950s. At the time, sociology was dominated by North-American functionalist theories of social reality which had been abstracted from the study of American society and which were taught not only at universities in the United States but in Europe and other parts of the world as well. For the great majority of sociologists, the study of social phenomena was the study of the American social system. The newly independent countries may have been in the majority among the world's nation states but, even though sociology had a major contribution to make to their analysis, they were of little interest to the generality of sociologists.

It is, of course, true that courses in the 'sociology of development' were introduced within the sociological curriculum, that several textbooks on the subject were published and that a good deal of sociological (and anthropological) research into the developing societies had been undertaken. But these activities were peripheral to mainstream sociological concerns and attracted relatively little attention from other sociologists. In spite of the gradual formalisation of the sociology of development as a specialism, it remained a minority interest within the discipline. The same may be said of anthropology, which is increasing overlapping with sociology. Although the ethnographic explorations of anthropologists have brought them into close proximity with development problems, much more needs to be done if their research is to be routinely applied to development policy problems.

An indication of the neglect of the subject in sociological circles is the lack of a distinctive sociological conception of development. In spite of their use of sociological concepts and attempts to relate sociological ideas to Third World issues, sociologists have been largely dependent on explanations of development derived from economic considerations. As was noted previously, economics provided the first systematic accounts of the causes of economic backwardness and prescriptions for the acceleration of economic growth and, like other social scientists, sociologists reinforced the way economists defined the subject. Studies of social structure, cultural institutions, behavioural attitudes, the family and other social phenomena in the developing societies, were subordinated to economic considerations and focused largely on the question of how these social realities impeded economic progress and the drive to modernisation. Implicit in this search was the notion of traditionalism as an impediment to economic development; this idea suggested that the introduction of technology and the promotion of industrialisation was hindered by the persistence of old cultural values and archaic practices. These studies conformed to the dominant view of development as an economic process which, as Apthorpe (1970, p. 8) put it, 'will run more smoothly if social lubricants are added to the machinery or if social grit is flushed out'.

The paucity of sociological involvement in development is revealed also in the fact that sociological knowledge was frequently applied to enhance the study of economic development by individuals who were not sociologists by training or profession. As de Kadt (1974, p. 1) put it, '. . . development economists have often incorporated their own do it yourself sociology'. Indeed, two of the most important 'sociological' accounts of development in the modernisation tradition were formulated by Hoselitz (1960) and Rostow (1960), neither of whom were working as sociologists. Another, by Hagen (1962), drew extensively on both sociological and social psychological ideas and was widely adopted in sociology courses even though the author was, at the time, Professor of Economics at MIT. The influence of Parsons, the leading exponent of American functionalist sociology, on the work of Hoselitz is, of course, profound. This is equally true of the impact of evolutionary sociological historicism on Rostow. But it is an indication of the neglect of development in sociological circles that the application of these sociological theories should have been applied to development issues not by sociologists but by economists.

It is often believed that the demise of the modernisation paradigm and the ascendancy of international structuralism gave greater scope for sociological involvement in the field. The popularity of neo-Marxian international structuralist accounts of the dynamics of underdevelopment in sociological circles, and particularly among student activists in the 1960s, would appear to support this contention. But here again, the role of sociology in the formulation of this approach has been secondary. The early ECLA proponents of dependency theory were economists and their work is essentially economic in character. Frank (1967, 1969) himself trained as an economist and his writing is in the tradition of political economy rather than sociology. This is true also of his mentor, Baran (1957), and of subsequent neo-Marxian and Marxian conceptions of development such as those of Amin (1974) and Warren (1980). Indeed, it is not easy to identify the distinctive sociological elements in publications about the sociology of development which reflect the structuralist influence. In books by sociologists such as de Kadt and Williams (1974) and Alavi and Shanin (1982), and in similar works, sociological identity is subsumed under political economy fusing the critical insights of sociologists, historians, political scientists, economists and other social scientists. This is equally true of work undertaken within the intellectual framework of the classical Marxian revival.

The emergence in the 1970s of a more explicit concern with poverty, deprivation, hunger, inequality, landlessness and other social manifestations of underdevelopment would appear to be highly congruent with sociological interests. Sociologists had often criticised the economic dominance of development studies for its lopsided emphasis on economic growth as measured by GNP increases and its neglect of the human dimension. But again, the new focus on 'basic needs', 'redistribution with growth' and other issues in social development has been pioneered not by sociologists but by economists. The work of Myrdal (1970), Seers (1972), Chenery *et al.* (1974), Streeten *et al.* (1981) and many others who have advocated a major reappraisal of development concerns is rooted firmly in the traditions of neo-institutional economics.

But perhaps the most obvious manifestations of sociology's neglect of development is the absence of a significant role for sociology in the formulation, execution and evaluation of development policy. Although development is a multi-faceted phenomenon that is amenable to analytical speculation, normative evaluation and practical engagement, it is the connotation of direct intervention through policy-making and implementation that gives it a distinctive meaning. It is on this aspect that sociology has had comparatively little to say. The term *policy* is not listed in the indexes of the leading textbooks on the sociology of development and it is surprising that the term *development*, which does appear, is usually not widely referenced. While economists and administrative scientists have produced numerous textbooks that deal explicitly with development policy, no such literature exists within sociology. Unlike economics and administrative science, the idea of development as policy clearly has little appeal in sociological circles. It is, as de Kadt (1974) observed, largely because of their lack of relevance to development policy that so little attention has been paid to sociological theories and approaches.

This is not to deny that many sociological (and anthropological) studies of development policies, programmes and projects have been undertaken and that some sociologists (and anthropologists) have made an important contribution to the understanding of policy issues. One need only cite the work of British sociologists such as de Kadt (1982) in the field of health care, Dore (1976) in education, Long (1977) in rural development and Lloyd (1979) in housing to appreciate this point. In recent years, assessments of the impact of particular projects and programmes have been published with increasing frequency. But although significant, the work of these and other sociologists does not alter the fact that the majority of sociologists who have taken an interest in development issues have not dealt with them in ways that are of value to development policy organisations. Many studies of development programmes or projects have been critical assessments by uninvolved academics who have sought to expose the errors, inadequacies and negative consequences of policy decisions. Often formulated in esoteric academic terms and frequently nihilistic in flavour, they offer few constructive suggestions for improving the policy-making process so that future mistakes can be avoided. Some reach the unhelpful conclusion that all effort to improve the well-being of the deprived masses of the Third World are doomed to failure until the world capitalist system has been destroyed. One example is Burgess's (1979) assessment of self-help housing programmes which concludes that whatever policy-makers do to improve housing conditions, they invariably promote the interests of the ruling capitalist class. A similar mood of futility characterises sociological writings on the informal sector, land reform, small-scale industrial programmes and other policy initiatives.

Of course some studies have been of considerable value to development policy-makers and, in this regard, the work of development anthropologists has been particularly useful. Studies by Polly Hill (1957, 1963) and Thayer Scudder (1962) are just two examples of anthropological research that has influenced policy. But too often, these studies are not directly related to the policy-making task and they are frequently undertaken after policy implementation has begun, when it is too late to influence critical decisions. Mair (1984) pointed out, for example, that Scudder's research into the social consequences of the Kariba dam was not commissioned by the development authority and that it was only undertaken after the dam was completed. But it did have a considerable impact on the way later large-scale irrigation and hydroelectric schemes sought to manage their social effects.

It is also fair to recognise that sociologists are not entirely responsible for their lack of involvement in development policy. There has been a good deal of prejudice against sociological involvement on the part of the planners and administrators. Sociologists and anthropologists have often been regarded as a hindrance in development programmes or as being wasteful of scarce resources in project planning. Mair (1984) cites one cost benefit analysis study which concluded that the advantage of applying sociological expertise was not worth the delay it caused to the project. Many project administrators are not only ignorant of the contribution sociologists can make but fearful that they will introduce radical ideas and subvert their authority. But sociologists cannot be exonerated either. They need to convince development policy-makers that they have a useful role to play and must demonstrate in tangible ways that they have something positive to offer. Unfortunately, many sociologists have taken the opposite view, arguing that sociologists are of most value if they remain detached from development policy activities.

A good deal of sociological writing on development has been explicitly critical of policy involvement. This is partly a reflection of sociology's inability to resolve the problem of ethical engagement which, as was noted earlier, has plagued the discipline since its formative years. But it is also a function of the type of theoretical conceptions which sociologists have embraced when seeking to comprehend development phenomena. These have generally facilitated an attitude of policy detachment. In the 1950s, when sociologists concerned with Third World issues adopted conceptions of development based on functionalist and neo-classical theories, the implicit acceptance of the natural workings of the system and the ability of the market to promote prosperity through its own internal dynamics impeded policy-relevant inquiry. In the 1970s, when neo-Marxian ideas were ascendant, the notion of policy involvement was viewed as futile and unlikely to bring about 'real' changes or otherwise as being conspiratorially supportive of the wicked capitalist system. While the critical analysis of development policies is acceptable, engagement in the policy-making task is regarded as ideologically improper. Developmentalism becomes, not a synonymn for commitment, but a term of abuse.

Another more general factor that has mitigated against direct sociological involvement in development policy is the prevalence of the so-called 'enlightenment' approach to applied research. Some sociologists have argued that the discipline's findings should be disseminated in a generalised way so that policy-makers, administrators and even ordinary citizens are enlightened by its insights and take them into account in pursuing their everyday affairs (Janowitz 1971). The persuasiveness of this view in sociological circles has weakened the alternative 'engineering' conception of sociology's role in public affairs which is based explicitly on the notion that sociologists can function as professional personnel or consultants providing specific expert answers to technical questions. Compatible with the disdain for applied sociology, the enlightenment approach has gained favour and impeded the emergence of a coherent body of knowledge which can be applied to development policy issues.

The case for sociological engagement

Is there then a case to be made for a systematic applied sociology of development, which transcends notions of diffusing sociological insights in a general way and provides specific technical information for development policy purposes? Although many academic sociologists would answer this question negatively, claiming that the discipline's commitment to analysis and the production of pure knowledge is an overriding concern, there are sound reasons for advocating sociological involvement in development policy. The most obvious is that there is a real need for the application of sociological insights to development problems. The enterprise of development has long been dominated by narrow economic considerations which have emphasised industrial investment, the commercialisation of agriculture and the application of modern technology to the productive process, often to the exclusion of wider social concerns. This narrow conception of development as an essentially economic process has since been heavily criticised and a good deal of evidence has been produced to show that rapid economic growth does not of itself solve the fundamental social problems of underdevelopment. Equally important has been the recognition that development projects have social consequences which need to be properly addressed. As the failures of conventional approaches have been recognised, the need for a multidisciplinary approach that takes the 'human factor' into account has been more widely appreciated. The history of project planning is littered with examples of wastage, disruption and other negative consequences of neglecting to take human and other social factors into account. The lessons of the past have facilitated a greater recognition of the need to examine the social effects of projects and to anticipate their social consequences. Sociological knowledge is needed to broaden the scope of development studies and to transcend narrow economic and administrative assumptions.

Coupled with the need for greater sociological involvement is the fact that sociologists are increasingly being asked to participate in development activities. Although sociologists were in the past seldom invited to join development project teams, there has been a significant increase in their deployment. Much of the impetus has come from the aid agencies which now regularly request sociological inputs into their projects so that the social implications of project planning can be carefully assessed. There are also indications that more sociologists are finding employment as permanent staff members in governmental development organisations in Third World countries and in the international agencies.

However, as more development agencies recruit sociologists to work in a professional capacity, the need for a coherent body of knowledge suited to the tasks they undertake has become more urgent. The lack of such a body of knowledge has clearly been detrimental to these sociologists who, unlike economists and administrative scientists, are compelled to formulate their own conception of their task. The discipline has an obvious obligation to provide clear guidelines on which professional roles for development sociologists can be based. A coherent approach to development policy is required also to meet the needs of students who study sociology with the view of finding employment in development settings. Many students in the industrial countries are attracted to courses in the sociology of development because they wish to work in the developing countries as volunteers or professionals. Similarly, many Third World students take courses in the subject in their own countries or abroad with the hope of finding employment in developmentally related settings. Unfortunately, many discover that their academic education bears little relation to the actual tasks they are required to perform.

Apart from these practical considerations, there are sound academic reasons for advocating an engagement in development policy. Speculative inquiry is enhanced by a thorough knowledge of the real world and, in a field like development, which is infused with practical considerations, sociological commentaries on the subject are rendered more meaningful through a familiarity with practical issues. An understanding of the real world of policy also permits sociologists to appreciate the normative implications of analytical theories. Although, as Midgley (1984b) has suggested, the major development paradigms imply a policy stance of detachment, they do have normative implications. For example, while neo-Marxian international structuralism is critical of policy involvement, the New International Economic Order, the case for 'de-linking' and the advocacy of policy appropriateness are just some of the normative implications of this approach which are not made explicit in analytical accounts. Sociologists have a duty to make their preferences clear and to reveal the normative implications of their work.

A closely related problem concerns the ambivalent stance of theoreticians on the policy implications of their studies. Ostensibly committed to the pursuit of analytical objectivity, they nevertheless do have views on how best development can be promoted. Subscribing to the idea of ethical neutrality, sociologists who worked within the modernisation tradition in the 1950s and 1960s believed that the dynamic of change would automatically propel 'primitive' societies from traditional backwardness to modernity. But, at the same time, many were enthusiastic advocates of population policy, community development and village education, all of which, it was thought, would facilitate the process of societal transformation. Many were also, as Frank (1971) pointed out, supporters of American foreign policy attempts to contain the spread of Marxist-Leninism which had become the favoured ideology of radical, anti-imperialist movements in the developing societies. Ambivalence continues to characterise the writings of many sociologists of development today, even though their ideological commitment is very different from the proponents of the modernisation school. Although critical of 'bourgeois' liberal writers who advocate 'developmentalism', they simultaneously profess a concern for the misery that characterises the lives of the Third World's poor. Hoogvelt (1982) personifies this attitude in her declared commitment to a deterministic materialist conception of development but simultaneous regard for liberal progressives who 'have done as much if not more than the Marxists to put the world's poor on the map' (p. 214). Alavi and Shanin (1982) reveal a similar ambivalence in their concurrent denigration of 'developmentalism' and desire for progressive change through the application of sociological knowledge.

There is, however, a legitimate concern that a sociological preoccupation with practical issues will impinge on the discipline's scholarly mission. As Steifel *et al.* (1982) argued, there have been enormous pressures from national governments, aid agencies and the international organisations on social science disciplines to enhance their practical relevance. Similar pressures have been exerted on Third World universities to espouse a developmental mission. Although laudable, the orientation towards practical concerns has often diverted academic expertise towards contract research and salary supplementation, to the detriment of scholarly creativity.

The issue of sociological engagement in development policy also raises questions of professional ethics which sociologists have not properly addressed. Like other social scientists, professional sociologists may find that their involvement in development policy places them in difficult situations in which ethical dilemmas cannot be resolved readily. They may find that their research findings or professional judgements are in conflict with established organisational policies or the preferences of their superiors and that they are under pressure to conform. But it should be remembered that these problems are not confined to sociology. Other social scientists who serve as professionals in development organisations, and indeed all types of organisations, face problems of this type. They have not responded by avoiding the challenge of engagement but instead have met it, working through the political process to bring their contribution to bear on decision-makers. Instead of decrying the risks and using them as an excuse for non-involvement, sociologists need to learn to cope with the demands of organisational politics and to exercise political acumen in responding to these pressures.

This is not to deny the need for ethical standards that will guide sociological involvement in development policy. Indeed, there is an urgent need for sociology to address the question of ethics for professional practice in a systematic way. That sociologists have not done so with determination and unanimity is a reflection of the discipline's inability to recognise the fact that many more sociologists are working as professionals not only in development settings but in other applied fields as well. The lack of a clearly formulated system of ethics does little to enhance sociology's standing and claim to recognition.

Towards a policy-relevant development sociology

While the case for more systematic sociological engagement in development policy is persuasive, the problem remains that there are no clear guidelines for an applied sociology of development or standardised job descriptions on which sociologists concerned with development policy can base their professional roles. It is beyond the scope of this chapter to provide a definitive statement on the subject. Indeed, it may be argued that a proper and considered formulation of the nature and scope of sociological involvement in development policy must evolve gradually as sociologists find their way about the field and as increasing opportunities for sociological participation permit a proper debate on the subject. But, in view of the more frequent deployment of sociologists in development programmes, there is a pressing need that at least some directives for professional engagement be formulated. There are indeed, certain elements of an applied sociology of development that can be identified. These relate firstly to the actual tasks sociologists perform in development settings and, secondly, to the discipline's academic content. A proper consideration of sociology's engagement in development policy is predicated on a consideration of what sociologists actually do and what their training equips them to do. Both invariably determine the nature of sociological involvement in the development policy task.

As has been suggested already, sociologists are increasingly finding employment in development settings and it is clear that any account of their contribution to the field must be cognisant of their actual roles and responsibilities. Although there is, as far as can be ascertained, no substantive information about the present numbers of sociologists who work in development settings or about the tasks they are required to perform, impressionistic evidence suggests that, as a more balanced view of development has gained currency, opportunities for the employment of sociologists have increased. There is an urgent need for research into the actual tasks sociologists in organisations concerned with development policy undertake. These tasks should be documented, evaluated and discussed since it is with reference to the real world that a considered conception of sociology's proper role in development policy must be based.

There are indications that major opportunities for sociological involvement in development are being created by aid agencies, primarily in the field of project planning where sociologists are now frequently called upon to assist in the collection of data, the assessment of needs, the determination of obstacles to implementation and the anticipation of the social consequences of the project. At this level of engagement, the sociologist's role is becoming more defined. Despite continued obstacles (as Hall shows in Chapter Two) and although there is a serious dearth of literature on the subject, many aid organisations have, through their experience of using sociologists, identified specific tasks and responsibilities for sociological personnel. In addition, the increasing utilisation of sociologists in development projects, primarily as short-term consultants, has provided greater scope for the application of sociological insights to development problems.

Sociologists also find employment at other levels of intervention and here their roles are less clearly defined. These include settings such as municipal and provincial administration, national government, and of course the international development organisations, both official and voluntary. Openings for sociologists have also been created in commerical consultancy firms but these are few in number. At these different levels, sociologists often work as permanent staff members with distinctive professional responsibilities. Although a degree in sociology has long been an acceptable qualification for employment in these agencies, sociology graduates in the subject have generally not been used in a professional capacity but rather as generalist civil servants and administrators. There is, however, a growing tendency towards identifying specialist professional roles for sociologists within these organisations. But here again, the literature on the subject is seriously deficient.

In some settings, such as urban development and national planning, more information about the tasks sociologists perform is available. In urban planning, sociological involvement in data collection, undertaking attitudinal studies, and advising on the location of social amenities has increased significantly in recent years. The engagement of sociologists in projects which seek to facilitate greater community participation in development has also increased (Midgley *et al.* 1986). At the level of national planning, a considerable emphasis has now been placed on integrating social sectoral objectives with national economic development goals and on assessing the welfare outcomes of planning decisions (Hardiman and Midgley 1982). Here the scope for sociological involvement is considerable. But, while openings for sociologists in national planning agencies have increased, the field is still dominated by economists. In this regard, it is depressing to note that sociologists have made a negligible contribution to the application of poverty lines to the planning task. Although sociology has a long-standing expertise in the field, having pioneered poverty surveys in the late nineteenth and early twentieth centuries, it is economists rather than sociologists who now employ these techniques to measure Third World poverty and to assess the impact of development plans on levels of living.

In addition to an assessment of what sociologists in development settings actually do, an account of sociological engagement in the field must concern itself with what the discipline's academic content trains them to do. Although it would appear from what has been said already that the content of academic sociology is ill-fitted to the development task, the discipline's potential for generating appropriate knowledge is considerable. It is not only a question of what should be applied but of how it should be applied. Sociology has collected a vast store of factual information which can be tapped but it is equally important that sociologists be familiar with methodological procedures that facilitate the production of knowledge and its application to development policy issues.

In this regard, sociologists who engage in development policy must be conversant with the sources of appropriate information which can be readily consulted to provide insights, if not ready-made answers, to specific problems. They must also know the procedures of research, observation and deduction which permit the collection and synthesis of information. Indeed, as Bulmer argues in Chapter Three of this book, sociologists can make an important contribution to development policy through applying standard sociological research techniques to the task of collecting, analysing and interpreting factual information.

As in other subjects, much sociological expertise about development comes from the experience of working in the field and from learning both by mistakes and achievements. While experience cannot be taught in the classroom or culled from the literature, sociology does provide its students with a sensitivity to social issues and an intangible 'feel' for its subject matter that is not always present in the other disciplines. This intuitive *verstehen* is another vital aid in the sociologist's intellectual armoury which is pertinent to the understanding of development questions. The same may be said of anthropology which, as Mair (1984) observed, is particularly well-suited to project planning, especially in rural areas. In offering advice, 'They rely on their general understanding of small-scale rural societies . . .'. Although sociologists do not claim any special expertise in understanding rural communities, they do have the training to view development policies from the perspectives of ordinary people whose lives will be affected by the changes that are introduced (Long 1977).

Sociologists who are concerned with development policy must be fluent in the three major tasks of analysis, evaluation and application since all are relevant to the sociologist's role in development settings. Sociologists concerned with development need to engage in analytical inquiry in order to formulate views of the development situation and to understand and interpret these realities. In this regard, they treat development phenomena in the same way as other categories of social reality. Sociologists should also engage in normative evaluations of development policy, seeking to determine the extent to which these policies conform to declared evaluative criteria. In this approach, sociological engagement in development becomes infused with moral notions concerning the desirable or undesirable social effects of development effort. Another aspect of the normative study of development concerns the production of sociological accounts that provide ideal typical statements of the end state of development effort and prescriptive formulations of how it can be realised. Finally, sociologists must participate in the direct application of sociological knowledge to development policy matters by becoming involved in the actual policy-making process and in its implementation. Sociologists need to understand the policy-making process, bring sociological expertise to bear on the decisions that are taken and be able to monitor implementation. Ideally, these three activities build on each other. Analytical inquiry provides a foundation for normative evaluation and this, in turn, permits the application of normative knowledge to policies, programmes and other practical tasks.

Sociology has an established capacity for analytical enquiry, providing a powerful set of conceptual tools for understanding and interpreting social situations. Analytical insights of this kind are determined in part by the sociologist's familiarity with macro-conceptions of development, such as the development paradigms which were described earlier. These provide a coherent view of the social world by organising perceptions of reality. Like other social scientists, sociologists cannot operate in an intellectual vacuum and are dependent on analytical schema that frame their observations as well as the actions they adopt in an attempt to modify that world. However, in spite of the importance of the discipline's analytical resources, sociology is characterised by a serious lack of normative theory on which to base evaluative judgement. Although, as was noted earlier, speculative sociological models do have normative implications, these are implicit rather than explicit and do not generally address policy concerns directly. Nor do they provide a systematic body of normative knowledge on which technical policy decisions can be based. In economics, where normative models have been greatly refined over the years, policy concerns are more readily addressed. Although sociologists are able to assess the likely outcomes of development policies by employing the generalised insights of the different paradigmatic conceptions, there is a need to relate them much more explicitly to evaluative concerns.

In applying sociological knowledge to the development task, sociologists need to be familiar both with the processes of policy-making and policy implementation and with the standard techniques that are used in development agencies as aids to policy-making, since it is through their ability to participate as political actors that their recommendations, professional opinions and expertise will be applied. The provision of sociological knowledge to decision-making is not sufficient to ensure its adoption. Although, as was noted earlier, a number of sociological studies of the failures of development projects have been published, their findings need to be applied in policy situations if they are to be of any value. To ensure the adoption of sociological expertise, sociologists must be schooled in the techniques of persuasion and negotiation that characterise organisational practices and facilitate the acceptance of particular viewpoints. But here again, as a consequence of the disdain for practical matters sociologists are, by training, ill-prepared for the task. Too frequently sociological advice is sought only after the implementation phase has been reached or when serious problems have been encountered. Sociologists must not only learn to sell their ideas but to ensure their timely engagement.

There are of course many other aspects of sociology's involvement in development policy that have not been dealt with here. Nevertheless, it is hoped that these ideas do at least point the way towards the more effective deployment of sociologists in the field. A consideration of the actual roles sociologists play in development policy settings and an assessment of the contribution of analysis, normative evaluation and the application of sociological knowledge may help to foster the emergence of a coherent approach to development as a sociological task. In view of the need for greater sociological insights into development policy, it is a task that requires urgent attention.

Sociologists and foreign aid: rhetoric and reality

Where are the sociologists?

Sociologists have been conspicuous by their absence from the corridors of foreign aid institutions. The evolution towards a multidisciplinary approach to aid-funded development activities within the past fifteen years or so has not, somewhat paradoxically, been accompanied by a corresponding emphasis on sociological inputs. The sad fact of the matter is that, despite a widening of the hitherto narrow, technocratic philosophies prevalent during the 1960s and early 70s, sociologists (and related specialists such as anthropologists) have not been consulted nearly as much as the rhetoric of aid policy-making would have us believe. The actual participation of sociologists in project and programme implementation, as well as broader policy issues, remains relatively small-scale and clearly inadequate. In spite of the many laudable arguments from official aid bodies in favour of social analysis as an essential prerequisite for the successful application of other technical and organisation inputs, few institutions have put this into practice on a significant scale and none has put the 'social dimension' on an equal footing with economic and other apparently more 'technical' aspects.

In this chapter the role of sociologists/anthropologists within aid organisations will be examined. Various explanations will be offered for their limited participation when compared with other experts such as economists, agriculturalists and engineers. These include academic, institutional, political and practical reasons. After illustrating how sociological expertise has been successfully applied to aid-funded development work, it is suggested that this role could and should be greatly expanded. However, before this goal can be realised, a number of preconditions will have to be met by aid organisations, by client governments and, not least of all, by sociologists themselves.

Sociologists in aid institutions: historical and contemporary roles

Applied research on development issues has been dominated by economists who, along with politicians, government planners and aid administrators, have become the main policy-makers. Historically speaking, sociologists and anthropologists have not played a major role in policy formulation. During the colonial period, for example, the first applied anthropologists advised authorities in dealing with cultural conflicts. The US, British and French governments all made some use of ethnologists in an attempt to reduce friction with indigenous populations (de Garine 1978). A landmark in the growth of applied anthropology was the foundation in 1926 of the International African Institute (IAI) which, according to Malinowski, was to be instrumental in 'bridging the gap between theoretical anthropology and its practical application' (Grillo and Rew 1985, p. 10). The Colonial Social Science Research Council was set up in 1944, a branch of the Colonial Research Committee, with anthropologists featuring largely in its membership, whose purpose was to fund applied research in the colonies and to provide guidelines for projects in specific sectors (Grillo and Rew 1985).

Yet although these links between British anthropologists and officialdom were established in an attempt to make the system of indirect rule more effective, it is questionable how much real influence they ever exercised on policy formulation. Anthropologists themselves were often reluctant to become too deeply involved in this field. Malinowski noted, for example, that although the ethnographer could advise, 'Decisions and the practical handling of affairs are outside his competence' (quoted by de Garine 1978, p. 57). For various reasons, which are discussed in greater detail below, the post-war period was marked by increasing disenchantment among anthropologists with the validity of their involvement in official activities, and a corresponding return to the purely academic environment.

There are still relatively few sociologists or anthropologists working in foreign funding agencies. During the 1960s this fact seemed to be rationalised by donors on the grounds that assistance was directed mainly to infrastructural projects such as transport, communications and power which were assumed, implicitly at least, to have little or no direct 'human' impact. The major funding agencies only demonstrated systematic concern for wider social issues in the 1970s, the UN Second Development Decade, stimulated by, amongst other factors, the tragic Sahelian drought of 1972–74 and the growing realisation that increases in Third World GNP had been accompanied by increasing poverty, both absolute and relative, in many countries where the benefits of development had not been adequately shared. The major breakthrough was perhaps the World Bank's 'poverty-focused' approach from 1973 onwards[1] which was paralleled in Britain in 1975 by a White Paper advocating an 'aid for the poorest' strategy. Other nations which followed suit included the Scandinavian countries, the Netherlands and Switzerland (Elliot 1982).

It was this trend which brought about a growing realisation of the need to involve sociologists and anthropologists in designing, executing and evaluating measures designed to benefit specific 'target groups' of poor rural producers and urban dwellers. To all intents and purposes, it was only in the mid-1970s that a start was made in recruiting sociologists onto the permanent staff of funding agencies and greater use made of short-term consultants. It had become clear that, even leaving aside considerations of humanitarian concern or social justice, the economic success of development schemes depended as much upon appropriate forms of social organisation and investigation as on efficient technical inputs. They were seen for the first time as mutually interdependent. Initially, of course, sociologists and anthropologists played a marginal role and were called in to diagnose faults in existing projects in the hope that such fresh insight would produce the solutions that had evaded their more technocratic colleagues. Only latterly have sociologists become more fully integrated into the whole project cycle, the point having been made over the years that careful consideration of social variables and repercussions is essential from the outset rather than simply as an afterthought.

Multilateral aid

At the forefront of this trend among the multilateral aid organisations has been the World Bank, following its policy shift in the mid-1970s towards a poverty-oriented approach in which the target group concept 'required a better understanding of the social stratification, culture, self-defined needs and social institutions of the beneficiary populations' (Cernea 1982, p. 127). The World Bank appointed its first full-time sociologists in 1974 for agricultural and rural development projects. This number has now been increased to about ten. There has also been a substantial increase in short-term consultancies by sociologists, rising from thirty in the three years from 1971 to 1973, to 184 in the five years from 1974 to 1978. Furthermore, these inputs have not just been at the appraisal and evaluation stages, but also in monitoring the implementation of projects (Cernea 1982). Considerable efforts have also been put into drawing up guidelines for dealing with social aspects of projects, particularly in the areas of irrigation, resettlement, livestock development, fisheries, forestry and, more recently, environmental conservation and rural roads (Perret *et al* 1980; Pollnac 1981; Cernea 1985; World Bank 1984).

Yet despite the large increase in lending to projects affecting poor groups and the publicity afforded to the Bank's concern for social analysis, the current use of sociological expertise is inadequate. On the Bank's own admission, 'Even though the number of Bank staff sociologists and consultants has increased in recent years, there are certainly not enough to assist on all projects.' Furthermore, as evidence perhaps of the low esteem in which sociologists still appear to be held by other professionals, 'when a choice has to be made between a technical consultant or a sociologist, the sociologist is usually left behind' (World Bank 1982).

However, in spite of these shortcomings, the World Bank's record on the use of sociologists and anthropologists is excellent compared with other multilateral bodies such as the Inter-American Development Bank (IDB) and the EEC's aid fund. The IDB has only one full-time anthropologist on its staff while the EEC boasts no such specialist, in spite of the fact that both organisations devote substantial portions of their budgets to rural development and urban poverty projects. The IDB does, however, utilise a 'socio-cultural checklist', introduced in 1984, to be used by client governments in the preparation of project applications as well as by Bank staff on mission (IDB 1984). Other important multilateral donors such as the FAO, the Asian Development Bank and the African Development Bank also have poor records in this respect.

Bilateral aid

A similar pattern is found with regard to bilateral aid. Sociologists and anthropologists are few and far between and, when they are found, take second or third place in the hierarchy after other types of technical expertise. There is, however, some cause for optimism and it is possible to cite cases of aid institutions which have taken steps to integrate sociologists/anthropologists into the various stages of the project cycle. The Swedish International Development Agency (SIDA) has been an outstanding example of this process in operation (see below). Another instance is the British Government's Overseas Development Administration (ODA), which at present has two full-time Social Development Advisers at its London headquarters, two Technical Co-operation Officers (TCOs) performing a similar role in regional offices around the world, and a Co-operatives Adviser. In addition, an increasing number of short-term consultant sociologists is being hired, a trend which is expected to continue. This apparent preoccupation with social issues was not, however, translated into specific guidelines on sociological aspects of project work until as late as 1982, when a document emerged stressing distributional questions, the implications of local social structures for project design, and community participation (ODA 1982). Subsequent publications have also emphasised the role of social factors and the problems which have arisen from past failures to give them adequate consideration (ODA 1983).

Another major bilateral donor which gives consideration to social aspects of its projects is the United States Agency for International Development (USAID) with its 'Social Soundness Analysis' guidelines, issued in 1982 (USAID 1982). These examine the compatibility of the project with the socio-cultural environment, the spread effect of new practices, the social impact and distribution of benefits, and the extent of participation by the poor in the development process. Yet in spite of some progress in this field the general picture in terms of sociological or anthropological contributions to aid-funded development work has been one of 'too little, too late' and, one might be forgiven for adding, 'still not nearly enough'. This is no accident and may be explained by a variety of factors.

As a starting point it has to be said that a major tenet among academic sociologists and anthropologists has been one of neutrality and non-involvement in practical policy issues. The long sociological tradition suggesting that a 'value-free' and 'objective' or detached study of society without a normative commitment is possible still holds wide acceptance in academic circles despite firm rebuttals of such a position (Myrdal 1962). As Midgley has shown in Chapter One of this volume, there is still a strong distaste amongst many social scientists for any activity which suggests 'social engineering' or the manipulation of behaviour towards predetermined ends. As will be traditions, it is also due in part to the disillusionment of many sociologists and anthropologists with their unsuccessful experiences in the field of applied social science.

The rationale of sociologists' non-involvement

Professional integrity
While rejecting the purist view described above and accepting the potentially constructive role that sociology and related disciplines such as anthropology can play in promoting human welfare there is often justification for such disquiet. Many committed social scientists engaged in development programmes gain the distinct impression that their prime function in the eyes of their employers is to remove 'inconvenient' social obstacles which threaten to block the smooth and speedy execution of schemes, regardless of moral or humanitarian considerations. Thus, some quite rightly refuse to have any dealings with activities which they see as an affront to their integrity. As long ago as 1938 Firth raised such ethical considerations. 'If the anthropologist is asked to help make a policy of Indirect Rule more efficient, is this with the ultimate objective of fitting natives for self-government . . . or . . . is it with the aim of simply getting a more cohesive community within the framework of an imperialist system?' (quoted by Grillo and Rew 1985, p. 14).

More recently, Leach has described development anthropology as 'a kind of neo-colonialism' (quoted by Grillo and Rew, 1985 p. 19). Many sociologists and anthropologists have eschewed a practical role for themselves in newly independent countries on the grounds, presumably, that they would simply be used to perpetuate the interests of ex-colonial and Third World governing elites, viewed as hostile to the types of progressive policies advocated by social scientists which involve a commitment perhaps to structural change and redistributive policies that would directly benefit the poorest and most exploited groups. As evidence of the dangers which accompany consultant aid missions to Third World capitals, Horesh cites the case of Ghana in the 1950s and early 60s where the government recruited foreign specialists to legitimise the preconceived strategy of rapid industrialisation. Only by withdrawing from policy-making, Horesh argues, can the expert maintain his integrity intact and be 'free of the normative constraints imposed by his clients' (Horesh 1981, p. 617).

Technocratic planning

If sociologists and anthropologists have tended to distance themselves from policy formulation and implementation for reasons of academic neutrality, to retain their integrity or from a desire not to endorse token reforms, then the aid organisations themselves have not tried sufficiently hard to break down these barriers and bring a larger number of such social scientists into the fold. Development planning has been characterised by a technocratic approach, particularly during the 1960s, but this is so even today when the emphasis on poverty-oriented projects would have suggested a much greater sociological input than is actually the case (Hall 1986). Aid institutions are staffed overwhelmingly by technical advisers who remain largely, if not entirely, insensitive to the wider social repercussions of their work. Economists, agriculturalists, engineers and hydrologists, etc., with a few notable exceptions, place technical achievements expressed in quantifiable terms well above the less easily manipulated and statistically definable social parameters of development. The academic community must accept its share of the blame for this situation, since the lack of co-operation and understanding between sociologists and economists at university level is legendary, and it is hardly surprising therefore if these attitudes are transferred to the non-academic sphere.

Poor training for development

At least part of the reason for the failure of aid technocrats to fully recognise the potential contribution of sociologists has, however, nothing to do with professional rivalry, narrow-mindedness or mis-understandings. The simple fact is that, due to their exclusion from practical development problem-solving, sociologists and anthropologists have not had the opportunity to develop the full range of skills required of them to transform their theoretical knowledge into policy-oriented research methodology (Almy 1979). Their lack of exposure to development and aid agency activities has created something of a 'Catch 22' situation, a vicious circle which is only just beginning to be broken. This is not helped by the fact that applied sociologists require special abilities which are not, on the whole, taught in university postgraduate courses. Furthermore, given the relatively lengthy time scale for producing written work under which academic sociologists and anthropologists normally operate, many find it extremely difficult to adjust to the constraints imposed on consultants. Perhaps more importantly, though, they find it hard to produce those neat packages of non-controversial recommendations which earn the praise of employers and client governments alike.

Institutional obstacles

Some observers have suggested that social scientists should adopt a more aggressive and commercial attitude and create a demand for their services rather than waiting for such a demand to emerge (Howery 1984). Yet the view that opportunities for sociologists to work as consultants are there for the taking if only a more forceful stance were adopted is surely over-simplistic. Notwithstanding the undoubted shortcomings of sociologists and anthropologists in several respects, the major reason for their limited participation lies not in their own defects but in the ideological and institutional obstacles within aid bureaucracies themselves.

It is perhaps legitimate to claim, as some have done, that during the 1970s when poverty-oriented development was in its infancy, the simple lack of an institutional mechanism for recruiting sociologists was a major reason for their restricted use (Husain 1976). Yet this explanation will not account for these deficiencies nowadays, when such channels are there if required. A more likely organisational factor, as Cochrane argues in the case of the World Bank during the early 1970s, is that the power balance among departments is likely to be disturbed (Cochrane 1976). Even when sociologists are taken on, their ability to have a significant impact on decision-making is severely curtailed by internal constraints. This is more serious when, as Stavenhagen notes, 'our well meaning social scientist soon becomes enmeshed in bureaucratic red tape, administrative paper-pushing, political in-fighting and general lack of receptivity . . .' (Stavenhagen 1971, p. 341). Such difficulties are exacerbated by the fact that sociologists form a very small minority of specialists within aid bureaucracies. Until more non-economic social scientists are recruited as generalist advisers and administrators their influence will continue to be marginal.

The crux of the matter: fear of dissent

The major reason for the limited use of sociologists and anthropologists by donor agencies is essentially, however, a political one. They are fare more likely than other 'technocratic' professionals to reach conclusions and make recommendations at odds with the assumptions held by aid organisations and their client governments. Sociological and anthropological knowledge is frequently perceived by officials as dangerous or embarrassing, even subversive. Apart from being more willing and better equipped to discover social facets of development work which may attract unfavourable publicity and/or slow down project implementation, anthropologists and sociologists 'are likely to treat the customers themselves as part of the datum of the enquiry, and thus as part of the problem under consideration' (Grillo and Rew 1985, pp. 23–4).

In this sense, Firth has labelled anthropology as the 'uncomfortable science' while modern academics state that the 'Sponsors often get more than they bargained for' (Grillo and Rew 1985, p. 23). Another observer noted of the anthropologist, 'Because he has gained the confidence of the populations concerned by the development programme and uncovered their deep motivations, which he is sometimes imprudent enough to defend, the foreign ethnologist is considered a dangerous element by the national authorities' (de Garine 1978, p. 57). Although much lip service is paid nowadays to the consultation of 'target groups' and their participation in project design, agencies often feel uncomfortable about the closeness of the anthropologist to rural people as a participant observer. On the other hand, Pitt notes that the sociologist 'may be marginally more acceptable' since his or her contact through questionnaire surveys is not quite as close (Pitt 1976, pp. 2–3).

Instances of open discord between aid agencies and contracted anthropologists or sociologists are rarely publicised. One well-documented case, however, concerns that of a consultant anthropologist hired by the World Bank to advise on the POLONOROESTE project in north-west Brazil (Payer 1982; Price 1985). This is a $1.6 billion scheme to develop a large frontier area, which includes a 1,500 km paved highway and planned colonisation to foster commercial agriculture. The consultant accused the Bank of distorting and ignoring many of his recommendations concerning changes in the methods used by the government indian agency (FUNAI) to deal with the estimated 8,000 indians to be affected by the project. Subsequently, international pressure from social scientists and environmental groups did in fact lead to the temporary withholding of loan instalments pending the inclusion of adequate safeguards by the Brazilian Government.

Whatever the relative merits in this particular case, it does illustrate the point that, even though many professionals working for large international agencies are motivated by the most honourable of intentions, bureaucratic constraints and political pressures tend to suppress direct criticism of client governments' policies. Just as the staff sociologist may jeopardise his/her career prospects or status within the organisation by being too critical of colleagues, so the consultant may forefeit possible contracts by showing such dissent. Thus the likelihood or even the possibility that sociologists and others must sacrifice their professional integrity to make socially negative if politically acceptable recommendations acts as a strong disincentive to their closer involvement with development agencies. Conversely, the fact that sociologists and anthropologists are more liable than other technical experts to make far-reaching criticisms of official procedures probably conditions aid bureaucracies into adopting a cautious and defensive recruitment policy.

The value of social analysis
However, the relative exclusion of sociologists and anthropologists from aid organisations is lamentable in view of the postive contribution they have to make. Systematic social analysis, while no guarantee of successful project design and implementation, is becoming increasingly recognised as an essential ingredient. Initially this was confined to rather belated evaluation studies of 'failed' projects but, more and more, social inputs are contributing to project formulation and appraisal as well as ongoing supervision. In terms of increasing project efficiency this would seem to be a wise step forward for, as Kottak concluded after analysing sixty-eight World Bank projects, those which did include consideration of social issues had demonstrably higher economic returns (Kottack 1985). In other words, 'Not only does a failure to consider the social and cultural context of a project invite inappropriate project design at best (and user hostility at worst), but also it usually leads to projects that are ultimately ineffective, wanted neither by their supposed beneficiaries nor by the investing public agencies' (Cernea 1985, p. 323).

Numerous examples may be given of cases where sociological analysis has led to projects being redesigned and made more appropriate to local needs. The case is cited of a World Bank project in Africa which was reformulated to take account of unforseen labour shortages (World Bank 1982). Another rural development scheme in Nigeria, following sociological appraisal, had to be rethought to facilitate land transfers from one ethnic group to another (World Bank 1982). After a series of negative repercussions arising from forced resettlement in dam and highway construction schemes, World Bank sociologists prepared guidelines which require governments to improve the treatment of displaced persons (World Bank 1982). In addition, sociologists have recently been focusing attention on devising strategies for the improvement of beneficiary participation in aid-funded development projects (Uphoff 1985). A growing literature exists on the role of sociologists and anthropologists in many other sectors including social forestry, design of rural road projects, fisheries development, organisation of irrigation farmers, land settlement schemes and rural water supplies (Cernea 1985; Grillo and Rew 1985).

Although sociologists and anthropologists can influence project design, implementation and certain areas of policy, it is often suggested that they could perform a wider educational role within their respective aid organisations. This involves making other technical experts more aware of social dimensions of their work, and encouraging a cross-fertilisation of ideas (yet it should be remembered at the same time that sociologists and anthropologists themselves have as much to gain from this process as their other colleagues). This would, the theory goes, increase all-round sensitivity to social problems and thus broaden the narrow, technocratic bias prevalent in development planning. However, serious doubts must exist as to how far such an informal process would reap dividends unless this kind of mutual consultation is properly institutionalised. There are also dangers inherent in the belief that it is possible to persuade non-social scientists that they can become social experts overnight. Too many technocrats believe either that social issues are simply irrelevant, or that they can be dealt with on the basis of a little superficial knowledge and a dose of 'common sense' ideas which, although politically convenient, are recipes for project disaster.

Discussion has so far centred on the use of expatriate sociologists and anthropologists in aid organisations, yet it is also extremely important to encourage the use of indigenous experts. They often enjoy a number of advantages over their Western counterparts, namely a better knowledge of local language, culture and institutions, greater ease of communication with beneficiary groups and sometimes a more effective position from which to engage in political action in pursuit of developmental goals. There are also, naturally, problems and constraints associated with the use of local social scientists, such as a lack of professional preparation for undertaking applied research, cultural bias and distrust by their own governments on political grounds. It would be ideal if a greater share of the applied research burden could be shifted on to the shoulders of local experts who, with the right training, are possibly in a better position to draw up realistic proposals on the basis of their intimate knowledge of the problems and practical alternatives. This would also help to create more local autonomy and reduce dependence upon foreign expertise. However, although this has been successfully tried on occasion (Hardiman and Midgley 1978), it remains to be seen whether Western experts or their employers in the major aid organisations would be prepared to weaken their control over the gathering and processing of such information.

The need for change

It is now established beyond reasonable doubt that sociological and anthropological expertise have a constructive role to play in development aid implementation. The evidence of project failures which might have been avoidable through adequate social analysis, as well as the ever-growing call for such inputs, bear ample testimony to this fact. Yet, even in the face of such pressing need, we are unlikely to witness a substantial increase in recruitment, particularly of permanent staff, until certain preconditions are met. First and foremost is the requirement that aid agencies adopt a genuinely multi-disciplinary approach to project planning and policy formulation. The harshest critics maintain that agencies only make a token gesture towards this end and that the presence of a few sociologists is mainly a cosmetic exercise to 'elicit cooperation and diffuse opposition' from target groups (Payer 1982, p. 352). Even moderate observers have noted the relative lack of social analysis in relation to the volume of projects undertaken. Ayres, for example, observes that despite its anti-poverty stance, the World Bank has little to say in its project documents about the socio-economic characteristics of beneficiaries, and that there is much confusion over the distributional impact of Bank-funded schemes (Ayres 1983).

The contribution of sociologists in terms of their specifically technical skills must be recognised and institutionalised alongside those of other advisers. They should be contracted not just as specialists but also as generalists within aid agencies and integrated into the earliest stages of project and policy discussions. This should happen, not when there is already a heavy institutional commitment to particular interventions, and it is too late to modify or even bring about their abandonment should this be deemed necessary, but at the initial stages of project appraisal (Conlin 1985). One encouraging example of an agency which has successfully integrated sociological and anthropological expertise into its aid policy-making and implentation is that of SIDA, the Swedish Government's development agency. Through the Development Study Unit of the Department of Social Anthropology at the University of Stockholm, SIDA has since 1974 utilised expertise in social analysis during the design, monitoring and evaluation of its foreign assistance programme (Krantz 1980; Tobisson 1986).

If internal reform within agencies is a major prerequisite, universities also have an obligation to produce more applied sociologists and anthropologists capable of devoting their skills to the solution of practical problems. If more job opportunities within aid organisations existed for such graduates, this might help to overcome academic mistrust of 'social engineering'. The onus would seem to lie with the aid bureaucracies themselves to create more demand for applied sociological skills by making social analysis an integral part of every aid package. Such an exercise would also, perhaps, lend more credibility to the very concept of development assistance, which as we have seen, is treated by many in the academic field with scorn and distrust partly because of the fact that it so often ignores social realities.

At a time when foreign assistance budgets in the West are under constant threat of cutbacks, and when aid is increasingly allocated with commercial and geopolitical interests in mind, the prospects for greater social analysis in project activities do not, on the face of it, look encouraging. There is some slight cause for optimism if we consider the fact that more sociologists and anthropologists are being contracted, even if the total input is small in relation to the need. Furthermore, it does seem that the handful of social experts advising on aid policy are gradually making their presence felt and that this has led to the adoption of a more sophisticated and multidisciplinary planning approach. Yet until they acquire more decision-making power within their respective aid organisations, the cynical observer could perhaps be forgiven for thinking that sociological recommendations will remain at worst rhetorical embellishments to project proposals or at best of marginal importance to the mainstream of development policy formulation.

Notes

The author wishes to thank Michael Cernea, Eva Tobisson and Robert Chambers for information provided as well as valuable comments on an earlier draft of this chapter.

1   The turning point is generally agreed to be Robert MacNamara's Nairobi speech to the Board of Governors of the Bank on 24 September 1973. This was followed by a series of sector policy papers in the areas such as rural development, basic education, basic health and low-cost housing. Significant changes in Bank lending followed. From 1961 to 1965, seventy-seven per cent of all Bank lending was for electric power or transportation, but only six per cent for agriculture and one per cent for social services. By 1981, thirty-one per cent went to agriculture and rural development ($3.8 billion), about half going to poverty-oriented projects. See Ayres (1983).

3 *Martin Bulmer*

Sociological research and development policy

Sociologists, including sociologists of development, display an ambivalent relationship towards policy. On the one hand, the process of policy formulation and activities of government intervention form part of their subject-matter, and one variable among many to be taken into account in studying urbanisation, or village politics, or fertility behaviour or whatever the subject being studied. On the other, sociological theories of the grander kind are cast in general, abstract, terms, dealing with broad societal processes such as industrialisation, modernisation and indeed social development itself, within which policy may appear to have a lesser part to play. Compared to political scientists and economists, sociologists have focused somewhat less upon the specifically *policy* dimensions of development.

Yet as James Midgley suggests in Chapter One, sociology does have a great deal to contribute to the understanding of development processes and policy, enlarging the view of the arena within which action takes place and pointing to the specific contributions which sociology may make in revealing social variables which aid and impair the pursuit of particular courses of action. The aim of the present chapter is to focus upon methods of sociological research, in order to demonstrate the value of a sociological approach. It will consider the main methods of sociological research in the Third World – social surveys, intensive fieldwork, secondary analysis of existing data and evaluation research – and the best means of ensuring high-quality data. Particular problems encountered in Third World research are considered, together with means to improve the data collection process. One aim is to provide a sociological understanding of the data collection process, including ethical and political aspects. 'Sociology' is interpreted broadly to include one or two examples drawn from the allied fields of demography and social anthropology.

The treatment does not take the form of a method-by-method discussion, since excellent textbooks and anthologies exist discussing research methods in the Third World which cover these very adequately (see especially Warwick and Lininger 1975; Casley and Lury 1981; Bulmer and Warwick 1983; Peil 1982; O'Barr *et al.* 1973; Kearl 1976). Rather its focus is upon the uses to which different types of data may be put in the policy process, their strengths and limitations, and the interpretive contributions which a sociological approach has made to development issues. Certain general issues are first considered, followed by research considered as intelligence; as monitoring; as contributing to the understanding and explanation of underlying processes; and as evaluation.

Research and policy

Two general maxims may be said to underly a sociological research perspective upon development: 'All is not what it seems' and 'Seek simplicity, and distrust it'. The complexity of social phenomena and the difficulties of disentangling manifold causes of human behaviour are common generalisations about the subject-matter of the social sciences. Different disciplines resolve the problem in different ways. Economists are prone to constructing abstract models of strictly economic behaviour, eliminating 'noise' from non-economic factors by a convenient *ceteris paribus* clause. Sociologists, awkwardly, tend to insist that other things are not equal, and that there are sociological realities which act to falsify the neat premises or conclusions of economic theory, or of behaviour based on it. Polly Hill cites the case of a Ghanaian attempt in 1953 to reduce the indebtedness of cocoa farmers, whose farms had been devastated by swollen-shoot disease, on the grounds that debt was bad and ought to be relieved. In practice, local farmers colluded to deceive government officials, sharing the handouts from the Gold Coast Cocoa Purchasing Company and never being called upon to repay the amounts disbursed. She shows that in the eyes of rural farmers no pejorative connotations attached to debt, and indeed that in rural society debt is part of a complex system of borrowing and lending on the basis of personal relationships which entangles everyone and has many functions (1986, pp. 1–7, 83–94).

This critical sociological scepticism may be applied in the first instance to the policy-making process itself. The burden of a sociological approach is to suggest not simply that certain theories or models – notably those of economics – may be misleadingly oversimplified when applied to development problems, but that the answer is not simply to replace one model with another, more realistic, sociological one. For the policy process is itself bounded by uncertainty which derives from the nature of the policy-making. There is an overriding tendency, particularly in academic circles, to believe that the answer to making policies more effective 'lies in bringing more information, thought and analysis into the policy-making process' (Lindblom 1980, p.11). This is largely mistaken. Policy-makers are affected primarily by the political context in which they operate, which is made up of a variety of competing groups (including domestic pressure groups, senior officials of their own government, and international agencies like the IMF, World Bank, FAO or WHO) seeking to influence the outcome of policy. New knowledge is but one further element to add to an already boiling pot. Policy-making as a process of 'muddling-through' is at least as plausible as one of it being a rational, knowledge-driven process (cf. Bulmer 1986, Ch. 1). This is not to say that enhanced knowledge has no influence upon the way in which policy problems are handled but, rather, that this influence seems more likely to be indirect, diffused and slowly percolating into the awareness of policy-makers. Sociological studies of knowledge-utilisation (cf. Janowitz 1970; Caplan 1975; Weiss 1980) suggests that it is rare for social science knowledge to be used in a manner analogous to the skills of an engineer or doctor, to solve a discrete limited problem (such as bridge design) on the basis of technical skills (although, as Hall shows in Chapter Two of this volume, aid-funded development projects form one area where this is desirable and feasible). Much more characteristic is a gradual process of 'enlightenment' whereby social scientific understanding is spread through research, publication, dissemination in the media, and social learning by present and future policy-makers.

This is allied to two increasingly important, if seemingly commonplace, insights from the sociological literature upon policy. To formulate and promulgate a policy tells one little or nothing about the eventual outcome. 'There is many a slip between cup and lip.' Personnel at different levels within an organisation may interpret the execution of a policy in very different ways. The role of junior or 'street level' bureaucrats in translating a policy into action is significant.

There is thus increasing interest in the *implementation* of policy in the development field, testing rigorously whether the aims and objectives have been translated into reality (see Grindle 1980). A sociological approach can often play an important part in explaining the disjunction between aspiration and reality which may arise. There is also a small but growing number of studies which recognise that the discretion enjoyed by certain lower-level bureaucrats may play a significant role in determining the extent to which a policy is put into effect or not (cf. Lipsky 1980).

Population policies provide an apt instance of the general truth of these insights. Donald Warwick's study of their implementation in eight developing countries shows clearly what a critical role the bureaucracy plays in implementing a policy and shaping the specific directions it takes (1982). Bureaucratic structures installed to promote co-ordination may instead generate chaos or competition, or conversely informal relations between government officials and private bodies may facilitate a family planning policy even without an official policy. The commitment of implementers often varies widely across time and bureaucratic levels. Three levels are clearly distinct: a country's top leadership, including ministers, officials and senior programme officials; middle management such as district health officers and clinic directors; and field implementers, especially doctors, nurses, midwives and social workers working in family planning. Even if commitment to a family planning policy is strong at the first two levels, not much will happen if commitment is lacking at the third level:

Field implementers are often caught between the incompatible expectations of the bucreaucracy, the (local) community and themselves. Contrary to the assumptions of machine theory, they do not always resolve these conflicts and ambivalences in favour of the family planning program. Some do comply with the demands of their superiors, and sometimes they overidentify with these demands, but even there they may have to rationalize their actions to themselves. A second way of resolving attitudinal imbalance is to engage in covert resistance including minimal performance of the job, selective implementation, administrative abuses, mistreatment of clients, and quiet subversion of the program. Another route is withdrawal, whether in the limited form of absenteeism or the ultimate form of resignation (Warwick 1982, p. 153).

Other significant factors impinging upon how population policies turn out are the general culture of the society, the sway of local opinion leaders, and the responses of clients to the messages with which government sought to change their behaviour. Population policy provides a good test of the ability of policy to bring about change because it seeks to change behaviour on a large scale by persuasion and voluntary means (only rarely is direct coercion employed).

Ethics and politics in research

Population policy also exemplifies some of the ethical and political difficulties which can face the sociological researcher. The above generalisations about the problems in actually implementing policy are derived from empirical research, but carrying out that research is sometimes far from straightforward. In a fraught area like family limitation policy, prescriptive issues arise which may, if research is injudiciously framed, lead to charges of normative bias and methodological weakness. This was the case with so-called Knowledge-Attitude-Practice (KAP) surveys widely carried out under American auspices in the 1960s and early 1970s. Critics (e.g. Warwick 1983) charged that the presumption of those conducting the surveys was in favour of family limitation and that, partly as a result and partly due to methodological weaknesses, the malleability of respondents' attitudes and their willingness to alter their behaviour was considered exaggerated. In the conduct of field research into many development issues with a sociological dimension, explicit attention is needed to ethical and political ramifications.

Factors which need to be considered include the sponsorship of the research, the research topic, staffing of a research project and collaboration between different researchers (especially if some are Western and some local), negotiating research access, research design, and the interpretation and dissemination of results (Bulmer and Warwick 1983, Section VII). All of these may raise ethical or political problems. For example, Warwick's UN-funded study of the implementation of family planning programmes (1982, pp. ix-xiv) faced delays resulting from bureaucratic politics in trying to get clearance in three out of the four main countries studied. Another country it was proposed to include was vetoed by the local UN representative on the grounds that the topic was too controversial. At publication stage, the sponsor (the UNFPA) demurred at having its name associated with publication of the report, and also refused to distribute a popular summary of the results which the project co-ordinator had prepared for them.

Anticipating ethical and political problems requires a knowledge of the local political and social system and some awareness of the ways in which research may impinge upon it. For example, in negotiating access, clearance at national level is frequently not enough, but the path must be opened at the regional and local levels as well. Whether and in what manner permission is given – for example, by a village headman – can affect the way in which researchers are treated and the kind of data that they obtain. Field research upon members of ethnic minority groups can be particularly difficult if they have been oppressed or exploited by the wider society, if the research deals with sensitive issues for the group, if the group's leadership is divided or unco-operative, or when the group's previous experience of research has been negative. Examples may be multiplied (cf. Wenger 1987) but the point is that there is an important political and ethical dimension to Third World research. Sociologists and anthropologists have been most aware of this among social scientists.

Research as intelligence

It is now time to turn to the more specific uses of sociological research in development policy, beginning with intelligence. By intelligence is meant basic social and economic data which provide a picture of a society at one point in time, which is of use to policy-makers and which can inform policy-making. Modern societies are so large and complex that no one individual, or group of individuals, can possess knowledge of that society sufficient to form a picture of its condition. Resort is thus had to more systematic and extensive methods of enumeration and inquiry: the population census; the registration of vital events; the production of statistical data as a by-product of administrative process (usually referred to as 'official statistics'); purpose-designed social surveys of various kinds; and more intensive field investigations involving participation and residence in a locality. The first three of these tend to be the exclusive province of government, and it is to government that one looks for the provision of those types of data.

Problems with census data
Sociologists, among others, have made an important contribution to development studies by pointing to the limitations of some of these sources, and the need for purpose-designed investigations of an extensive or intensive kind. Censuses, however, well-conducted, have

inherent limitations. They are massive and costly exercises, which can only cover a limited number of topics and which cannot easily be expanded. The information to be gathered must be of the most simple and straightforward factual kind. Because of their size and cost they are usually only conducted every ten years. Data processing is slow, and results available only after considerable delay. Moreover, though not so flawed as to be useless, census along with registration data and official statistics need to be treated with critical scepticism by the social scientist, with due attention to the conditions of their production. Censuses, for example, are complete enumerations of a population at one point in time carried out by temporary enumerators recruited for the purpose – often local teachers, officials or students. (The most recent Chinese census required some six million *enumerators*.) They are given a brief training but, in the nature of the case, are unskilled in social investigation and data-gathering. The quality of the resultant data is thus variable and, while the order of magnitude of the basic population count is usually fairly accurate, one cannot look to the census in many countries for more refined data. In a few unusual countries even the basic count has been absent or suspect. Political problems in the Lebanon over ethnic and religious divisions prevented a census being carried out for many years, and in the last two decades the Nigerian census has been a live political issue, at least one set of results being cancelled as unreliable and others being of uncertain accuracy due to political inflation of the count (Mabogunje 1976). But these are exceptional cases.

Errors in official statistics
Administrative data are even more prone to unreliability, for they are produced by non-statisticians, with non-statistical objectives, as a by-product of administration. They need to be scrutinised particularly carefully since the imperfections in them may not immediately be apparent:

If a serious study of the availability of reliable data is undertaken, the situation in many developing countries is found to be quite alarming. It is not only a question of lack of data; in many situations, the position is more a case of poor quality data than of no data. Further, there are situations where data are available, but minimal or no use is made of the same owing to lack of proper infrastructure or suitable opportunities (Murthy 1978, p. 232).

Economics, particularly macroeconomics, tends to rely upon such official sources almost entirely, and to the extent that an economic analysis of development is the dominant approach, these data deserve particularly close scrutiny. For development economics is limited not only in its analytical framework (see Chapter One) but also in the kinds of data upon which it relies. These data include financial statistics, agricultural data, education, industry, trade, health, and transport statistics, and figures produced by public corporations concerned with agricultural marketing, port operations and power generation. The more important series are used by international organisations such as the United Nations, the World Bank, FAO and WHO in their statistical publications, and thus acquire even wider currency. Yet economists in particular tend to treat such data as relatively unproblematic, and to use it in preference to conducting their own inquiries for intelligence purposes. In preparing his extensive study of South Asia (1968), Gunnar Myrdal was unusual in concluding that any statistics available in the developing countries of Asia had to be scrutinised most carefully, for at best they were highly uncertain and not as specific as the analyst would desire.

Statistics of landholdings and crop yields may furnish an example of the possible fallibility of official data. Such data are regularly collected by government, often as a by-product of administrative process, as important data about the structure of rural agriculture. How reliable are they? Wolf Ladejinsky reported a field trip to India in 1969 in the course of which he met a Bihar landlord:

He first informed us that he owned 16 acres of land, but corrected himself under good humoured prodding of a crowd of farmers that he had failed to mention another 484 acres. The lapse of memory might have had something to do with the ceiling on landholdings and its maximum permissible limits of 60 acres, but, on the other hand, no owner bows his head in shame on account of ceiling evasion (quoted in Chambers 1983, p. 65).

A field research study in Tamil Nadu in India estimated that extensive enumeration methods underestimated the area covered by study villages by fourteen per cent at the listing stage and eight per cent at the farm survey stage, resulting in understatement of acreage under crops (Chinappa 1977). Hill (1986) suggests that village land records in Karnataka state were of very variable quality, partly due to landlords not reporting changes of ownership to the *panchayat* secretary, partly to the village focus on landownership and the exclusion both of plots held elsewhere by landlords and the exclusion of landless labourers (so providing an underestimate of the extent of the problem). The difficulties of official data are nicely captured in what has been called

Panse's Law, that the average size of landholding in a village increases with the length of residence of the investigator (Panse 1958). This is not to say that all such data are erroneous, but that they are prone to error and the errors are difficult to detect.

This is even more the case when information about the source of the data is lacking. A very experienced FAO statistician, S. S. Zarko-vitch, reports that out of 120 countries reporting crop production, eighty used eye estimates (i.e. informal guesses) in obtaining data on the yield of such important crops as wheat and maize, and that seventy-four and ninety-four countries respectively used subjective methods to estimate cattle and milk production respectively (1975). In Nigeria, domestic agricultural production was simply estimated by assuming that local food production increased as fast as population, on the ground that no noticeable changes were occurring either in food consumption per head or in imports (Rimmer 1982, p. 52). In fact in this case one error compounded another, since the growth rate of population was not known either (due to census problems) and this rate was an assumed rate also.

The investigator may suspect that errors exist in official data if inconsistencies can be discerned. Data relating to exports from and imports to particular countries may be discrepant, for example, the figures from one country not matching those of the other. Within countries, different departments in the same country may produce different estimates for key economic series, and even the same authority may report different measurements of the same item at different points in time. In some countries, this results from the weak statistical infrastructure and the poverty of the society. Writing of saharan Africa, Berg commented that the extreme weakness of statis-tical sources was unsurprising:

Not only are statistical units small and poorly financed in the Sahel, but the difficulties of generating acceptable data are immense. Everything related to external trade . . . is necessarily part fantasy, since so much of total trade . . . takes place unrecorded. The vital data on agricultural production, marketing, size of livestock herds are all spun from a thin web of skilled (and sometimes not so skilled) guesswork. It's the same with most other data (1975, p. 4).

Sources of error which are not immediately apparent are much more insidious and more difficult to detect. They may arise from a variety of sources (for an excellent discussion see Morgenstern 1963, pp. 3–60). These include falsification of information, both by observer or observed. Some of the difficulties with land tenure data derive from this source, deriving from the suspicions of the observed. A particularly insidious form of falsification by observers is the provision by officials of 'guesstimates' of, for example, crop yields in the absence of hard data based on actual enumeration or observation. Errors may derive from the lack of training of observers, notably officials who gather data as a by-product of administration, and census enumerators. They may be due to lack of clear definition or classification when data are being collected. The research instrument used to collect data – the statistical form to be filled in by an official, the census schedule, registration particulars – may be deficient and may lead to error. The coverage of the population studied may be incomplete. Health statistics derived from patients presenting themselves to hospitals or clinics exclude those who did not seek treatment. Censuses, although they aspire to one hundred per cent coverage, rarely achieve it in full. It is estimated, for example, that recent African population censuses have undercounted by a margin of error of between five and fifteen per cent (Rimmer 1982, p. 51). However well-intentioned those collecting the data, errors occur due to human fallibility at all stages of the data collection process.

The result is that data which appears pristine and authoritative upon the printed page, with the authority of government or an international organisation upon the cover, must be treated with circumspection. Even in such basic data as GDP errors cannot be assumed to cancel each other out:

The GDP, like many official statistical aggregates, is built up partly from precise and firm information, partly from information which is precise but unreliable, and partly from extrapolation, interpolation, imputation, the blowing up of sample data, simplifying assumptions and guesses. The result is a total for which a minimum margin of error of 10% must probably be assumed (Rimmer 1982, p. 53).

The conclusion to be drawn about the sociological contribution to gathering basic intelligence in developing countries is two fold. The first is negative, in the sense of pointing to the manifold defects which exist in official statistical series and to some extent the census, where indeed data about social and economic matters is available at all. These defects should not be exaggerated but neither, as they tend to be by economists, should they be played down. 'Such statistics are usually of far worse quality than their users purport to realise, and . . . it is commonly with their aid that economists, and others, do so much to mislead the world' (Hill 1986, p. 31). Secondly, more positively, such a sociological critique points to the need for purpose-designed inquiries, using social survey and ethnographic methods, to gather data at first hand for the particular purposes of inquiry. Such methods are briefly discussed under the next topic, monitoring, but they are much the most characteristic methods of sociological research in the Third World. Official statistics may be used as background data, and for comparison with survey results. Census and registration data provide important background information, and the census may in some circumstances be used as a sampling frame for a large-scale survey. But almost all sociologists of development conducting empirical research find it necessary to undertake first-hand investigations, so that they themselves can design the research, guide, control and participate in the collection of data, and themselves analyse the results.

Monitoring

The second type of policy-relevant research is monitoring. If intelligence sought a picture at one point in time, monitoring seeks to grasp a changing picture and follow changes in society over time, not just to know in what direction society is changing but, in crude statistical terms, what impact policies may have. Thus standard series such as per capita income or the crude birth rate may be used by governments as a highly simplified measure of their success or failure in achieving certain objectives. Monitoring may take one of several forms – social indicators; continuous social surveys; *ad hoc* surveys; ethnography; and more truncated forms of inquiry. These will be considered in turn.

Social indicators

The social indicators movement in industrial societies was an outgrowth of the space race between the USA and the USSR and a desire to monitor the rate of change in American society (cf. Carley 1981). In the Third World, social indicators became a means of improving the measurement of national welfare and an alternative to measures based on GNP as a yardstick for determining the extent of social progress. Their most salient use is in international comparisons of the type which appear annually in the World Bank's *World Development Report*. Critics of GNP as an indicator argued that it omits many important non-market activities, aggregates various activities purely in terms of money values (how does one place a monetary value on life expectancy?) and pays little attention to distributional issues. There has been a good deal of work done to try to develop alternative indicators of development, of which the Physical Quality of Life Index (PQLI) has been the most widely used. It is formed from three equally-weighted social indicators; infant mortality, the life expectancy of one-year-olds and literacy. These are available for a wide range of countries and seem to be relevant to development (Morris 1979). The PQLI has been sharply criticised on various grounds, and is as imperfect as GNP as a crude measure of a nation's progress. It is but one of a number of attempts to construct indices of development in terms of quality of life or levels of living (cf. Midgley and Piachaud 1984; Hilhorst and Klatter 1985; Miles 1985, Ch. 2). Almost all rest upon official data sources and suffer from the limitations of those sources.

Social surveys

Many Third World governments recognised the limitations of census registration and administrative data and initiated their own large-scale social surveys for planning purposes. The prototype is the Indian National Sample Survey (cf. Murthy and Roy 1983), one of the first of its type in the developing *or* developed world. Since then many countries have established multi-purpose continuous household surveys. Their advantages are considerable. Using probability sampling methods, a fraction of the population is contacted, greatly reducing the size, cost, geographical spread and fieldwork effort involved in the survey, compared to a census. Its smaller scale, moreover, means that trained interviewers may be used instead of temporary enumerators, so that the quality of data collected is higher. The use of face-to-face interviews, rather than household enumeration where the head of the household may answer on behalf of all members, also renders this a more flexible tool of data collection. Even so, formidable problems of non-sampling error remain. An international conference in 1977 drew attention to the importance of reducing non-sampling error, particularly through the better training of interviewers (OECD 1978). Estimates from African sources suggest that total non-sampling error is considerably greater than sampling error at most levels of interest (Ward 1983, pp. 131–2). The solution lies in using better trained field staff rather than increasing the sample size. Such an approach is congruent with the tendency in sociological research on development for the investigators to mount their own survey rather than rely on officially-derived data sources.

There are many subjects, in any case, on which data either from official statistics, censuses or continuous surveys are not available. The latter, which in principle can provide data on a range of topics, suffer from chronic problems of overload and cannot provide adequate rational estimates for a range of topics, particularly topics such as health or agricultural productivity which require careful and extensive questioning. Moreover, these sources are likely to be less useful for more local studies or studies of particular development schemes whose aim is to monitor change over time. For these purposes one option for the sociologist or demographer is to conduct their own survey.

An example of such an inquiry on a very large scale is provided by the World Fertility Survey, carried out in forty-two countries in the decade after 1972 at a cost of about $40 million, paid for by the UNFPA (Cleland and Hobcraft 1985). This was an exceptionally large-scale project and most survey work is conducted on a more modest, and local scale. Towards this other extreme, Hardiman (1984a) gives an example of a household survey carried out in Maiduguri in Northern Nigeria which aimed to establish the existing situation, indicate trends, and provide material for decision-making by the town-planning team for whom it was carried out. Its coverage included basic demographic data (in the absence of a recent census in the country); household size and composition with particular reference to the compound system of residence; patterns of and reasons for migration; housing tenure and land access; and people's views about housing and their neighbourhood.

This is not the place to describe the various phases of the survey process, and standard sources may be consulted (particularly Warwick and Lininger 1975 and Casley and Lury 1981). The point to emphasise is that the design and data collection phases of the inquiry are under the direct control of the investigators who, if they wish, may become heavily involved in the actual data collection themselves, as interviewers. This gives the investigators direct purchase upon the problem and the possibility of obtaining a 'feel' for the situation and world view of those being studied. This is particularly important where the social distance between investigator and investigated is wide, as in many village studies. Moreover, survey research in developing countries faces considerable problems in securing reliable and valid data (cf. Bulmer and Warwick 1983, Sections IV and V), due to difficulties in questionnaire design, multi-lingual standardisation, the language of the interview, the role of the interviewer, the perceptions of the respondent and the cultural milieu in which the interview is conducted. If the investigator is involved in the data collection process, these difficulties may be grappled with more effectively.

Participant observation

Surveys provide one means of monitoring the efficacy and impact of policy interventions. A different strategy may be to adopt the anthropological role or become a participant observer, living for a period in the milieu being studied, and studying the setting over a period of time. This permits a variety of techniques to be employed: local census-taking, informal interviewing, the use of informants, and direct observation of events, by means of which a total picture may be built up. Again, standard sources may be consulted (cf. Srinivas *et al.* 1979; Agar 1980; Burgess 1982, 1984) which describe the experience of fieldwork and its methodological aspects. This method, too, is widely favoured by sociologists. It has the advantage of getting close to those being studied, of eliciting a variety of information in a variety of different ways, of being able to be present on some occasions and observe action as it happens, and of coming to appreciate the world view of those being observed. This has yielded valuable insights not available through survey research and, on some subjects, more accurate information than that yielded by surveys. Ethnographic field research is, however, not without its difficulties. Such case studies cannot be representative of a larger entity – one Indian village is far from being a microcosm of Indian villages – so the generalisability of results is in doubt. Though there may be gains in the validity of data, reliability is an issue just as much as with survey methods. Indeed, the dependence upon a single investigator may increase the possibility of bias or selectivity in recording or interpretation. Re-studies of the same milieu are rare, so it is difficult to check the accuracy of the account provided.

Triangulation

Participant observers rarely rely upon one source alone, and 'triangulate' their sources, that is, they compare and cross-check information and interpretations provided from more than one source. This principle can be applied more broadly through multi-method triangulation. The monitoring of change rarely relies upon a single method, and it is not uncommon to combine ethnographic and one's own survey data with official statistics and perhaps documentary sources. Data which is confirmed by more than one source has a greater reliability than data from only one source. It is not always possible to triangulate in this way – the data may not be commensurate – but as a general strategy it has shown its value in sociological inquiries. For example, in his study of the socio-economic impact of government irrigation schemes in north-east Brazil, Hall (1978) used this method to good effect.

Rapid appraisal

Both survey research and ethnographic field research are time-consuming and expensive if conducted thoroughly. Not infrequently the investigator needs a quicker and more direct method of monitoring a particular policy or intervention. Here the pitfalls of superficial acquaintance loom. Chambers (1983) has described the phenomenon of what he calls 'rural development tourism', by which outside visitors from urban areas or from overseas are given brief, pre-planned visits to selected rural areas chosen for their adoption of progressive farming methods, their propinquity to urban areas, their entrepreneurial spirit, or a variety of other factors by which they stand out from the mass. Even if a village is not a showpiece, various biases can operate toward villages on a tarmac road, or near a main artery; to villages where projects are actually being implemented; to more affluent, male, rural dwellers; and to tropical rural areas in the dry season, when they are accessible, rather than the wet season when they may be less prosperous. Yet their is a need for methods which can yield useful results in a short space of time.

What has been termed Rapid Rural Appraisal (RRA) is more systematic than development tourism yet much quicker than a full-blown academic study. It attempts to use some of the principles of scientific investigation but adapt them to the short time period available. Chambers (1985) suggests the need to make full use of available information, particularly academic studies in the region or of the problem; the importance of learning from rural people and listening to them and their local knowledge; the need to use key indicators (such as the number of tin roofs in a village as a sign of relative affluence or poverty); and the ability to carry out *ad hoc* local research and observation, even if not a fully worked-out piece of research. Specific methods of investigation include informant interviewing, group interviews, informal interviews (balancing openendedness and direction) and aerial inspections and surveys, particularly when concerned with animals or certain types of natural resource. Doubt and self-criticism are essential components as a safeguard against superficiality and error. RRA is no substitute for a full-blown survey or piece of field research, but it is much to be preferred to 'development tourism' and the imperceptions to which it gives rise, as a way of monitoring change.

Understanding and explaining underlying processes

Where sociological approaches to development yield the greatest return, and provide a distinctive contribution, lies not so much in the data collected but in the use of that data to understand and explain development problems and analyse the impact of policy at a deeper level. Continuous surveys *may* perform this function, but have some difficulty in doing so. To trace the interrelationships between various factors – for example, between education and migration, or migration and fertility – is a complex matter, leading into difficult problems of explanation. Explanations of the existence of phenomena – for example, of the existence of poverty – are difficult and elusive, and when working with continuous survey data one can rarely specify in advance all the interrelationships to be examined. Initial hypotheses are refined or changed when first results are in as part of an iterative process. But the investigator is limited to the variables covered in the survey, and data analysis of an explanatory kind is likely to raise questions about relationships which can be answered by collecting additional data. A sociologist relying purely upon continuous surveys would be limited in the extent to which the theory could be explored.

Sociologists therefore commonly use in explanatory studies a mixture of survey methods and ethnographic field research. The types of explanation which are produced are varied, rarely corresponding to the very rigorous concept of a causal if . . . then . . . relationship, held in some natural sciences. But they do attempt to make sense of the phenomena being studied and to suggest possible determinants of the end-states. Particular interest attaches in policy research to variables which are susceptible to manipulation by policy-makers, but in development studies, where interventionism is common, almost as great interest attaches to variables which explain why policy interventions may fail to work.

A good example is provided by James Scott's study of Malaysian peasants and the impact upon them of more capital intensive agriculture, *Weapons of the Weak: Everyday Forms of Peasant Resistance* (1985). His general theme is that rural peasants are far from lacking in perception or intellectual resources, living in a slough of false-consciousness. There was in fact an active village culture of gossip, character-assassination, petty theft and obstruction waged by the weak against the strong. Economic change had recently hit the area with the introduction of irrigated double-cropping of rice and the use of combine harvesters. The benefits of this 'green revolution' had accrued mainly to the wealthier farmers who had, as a result, much less need to rent land or keep in with their poorer neighbours by feasts and charitable handouts. Yet though there is no disagreement about the economic facts, the ways in which local peasants interpret the impact of the green revolution does not derive from the economic reality. It is not explained fatalistically or in terms of Allah's will, or as the malevolent result of government policy: 'Instead, the poorer strata of Sedaka see the causes of their present distress as primarily *personal* (that is a result of human agency), *local*, and largely confined to the Malay community (Scott 1985, pp. 180–1). The use of leasehold tenancy and dismissal of smaller tenants is seen as stemming from landlord's desires for greater profits. Use of combines is a way of cutting labour costs and the trouble of hiring extra labour. Reduction in charity stems from a desire of the rich to protect their wealth:

> The more distant and impersonal causes that most assuredly play a role here are upstaged by a perspective that emphasises moral lapses, selfishness and the violation of social decencies. As the poor see it, the rich have callously chosen to ignore their obligations to their neighbours. How else are we to understand the tendency of the poor to focus at least as much on the disrespect and contempt they now confront as on the material losses they have suffered? (Scott 1985, pp. 181).

The poor understand the larger forces at work which are affecting the village, but focus upon local landowners because it is convenient to do so – they are most immediately responsible for recent reverses – and strategically to try to influence those from whom they have *some* claim to consideration, however tenuous.

Nor was action purely symbolic. The village had a gate from the main road, which was kept locked to bar access to lorries, partly to preserve the mud track and partly to ensure continued labouring work in transporting sacks of paddy from the fields to the road to be picked up by lorries sent by urban merchants. Incidents in which larger tenants unlocked the gate to allow lorries into their fields aroused fierce local indignation and protest, indicating a willingness on the part of village dwellers to undertake *limited* action. A study such as Scott's enables one to grasp the situation as it is defined by those on the receiving end of the development process – poor villagers – who have most to lose from agricultural modernisation.

Another case of the value of a sociological or anthropological view of a problem is provided by Barbara Harrell-Bond's study of emergency assistance to Ugandan refugees in the Sudan (1986). Here the problem of understanding is not that of grasping the different perspectives of rich and poor in the indigenous population, but in helping staff of Western donor agencies appreciate the world view and behaviour of inhabitants of refugee camps. Agency officials, preoccupied with the day-to-day existence of the living, could not understand why refugees attached such importance to burial of the dead. Yet this ignored the importance of observing traditional customs:

A proper burial is the most important act of respect which can be paid to the deceased. There is probably no greater disgrace to a family than to have failed to observe funeral customs. Many refugees are haunted with the memories of those relatives they left unburied in the bush while fleeing for their own lives . . . Even the children's drawings portrayed painful memories of the unburied dead . . . It is not enough to simply dig a hole and cover the corpse; it must be properly wrapped. Families would be willing to go to sleep hungry to find the money to buy cloth (Harrell-Bond 1986, p. 293).

African refugees have not only lost material possessions and support, roots, been moved geographically a long distance and torn from their cultural setting. They have also lost emotional support, and lost members of their family as a result of military violence, illness and malnutrition . As part of the study, a very small sample were administered the Present State Examination, a psychiatric research tool modified to test for depression and anxiety. The results were analysed by clinical psychologists, and three-quarters of the sample of fifty-seven suffered from appreciable psychiatric disorder. The presence of a spouse reduced the likelihood of being depressed, the absence of close relatives increased the likelihood of depression. Harrell-Bond concludes that humanitarian aid programmes need to consider the mental health of refugees and devote more attention to its treatment:

Policy-makers cannot afford to be ignorant of the traditions and customs of the refugee communities for whom they are planning programmes of assistance. If expatriate personnel continue to dominate implementation of assistance, then they must be adequately instructed . . . There is a need for general recognition that African refugees, like those elsewhere, are often psychologically disturbed by their experiences . . . Psychiatric medicine should be available to those who need it. At present, the usual approach is to prescribe Valium indiscriminately (Harrell-Bond 1986, p. 323).

Imposing Aid also contrasts self-settled refugee camps in the southern Sudan with those established by western humanitarian agencies. Though there are problems in the routes by which refugees reach each type of camp, a clear difference emerged. Those in agency camps had lost dignity and self-respect more markedly than those in self-settled camps. This appeared to be due to the way in which aid agencies operated. Logistics dictate (it is thought) a 'command' bureaucracy, for refugees are destitute and must be provided for. Consultation is not deemed necessary for delivering immediate assistance, but in the longer run lack of it is destructive of social skills needed for long-term rehabilitation. The study shows that relief agencies fail to interest themselves in the assessment and employment of skills possessed by camp inmates. Peasant farming is often set out as the rehabilitative goal for people with high degrees of technical skill. Agencies also may prefer to recruit poorly qualified expatriates rather than well-qualified refugees to help run the camps. Her study demonstrates how a sociological research perspective can show one part of the development process up as dominated by particular assumptions and perspectives, often of a technocratic kind, which are inappropriate to the social circumstances and structure of those affected.

In an account of irrigation systems in the Philippines and Sri Lanka, Coward (1985) emphasises the importance of using sociological analysis to understand the institutional and organisational dimensions – the social patterns of irrigation behaviour – and to help understand the existing pattern of water allocation, from which change is planned. This is no easy task, requiring a perceptive eye and theoretically-informed observation. In this case, the study showed that, while a statistical survey might suggest that there was a lack of co-ordinated effort to maintain the system and allocate water between landholders, in fact there was an elaborate social organisation both for allocating water and maintaining the system in both dry and wet seasons (between which there was considerable variation).

Evaluation research

Sociological research thus has much to contribute to understanding social circumstances and explaining the genesis of social conditions which it is the aim of development planners to modify or change. Even when focused upon policy, such research remains diagnostic, providing the policy-maker with clues to the problem, or telling him after the event why intervention did not have the results which were expected. Policy-makers also require feedback on how policies are working, one reason why evaluation research is of growing importance in the development field. Evaluation research may mean different things. One form is the large-scale social experiment, where rigorously controlled social intervention is designed to test the effects of particular policies (Bulmer 1986, Ch. 8). Another form is in effect a version of social indicators research. A third form involves the in-depth examination of particular policy interventions to explain their relative failure.

The first type, the large-scale experiment, is rare in development studies and will not be further discussed. More common is the use of continuous surveys carried out by government, though these are most suitable for national policies carried out over an extended period of time, where there is the opportunity to collect adequate baseline data, secure adequate geographical coverage, and follow changes in the policy-dependent variables over a period of years. Continuous surveys are less satisfactory if one wishes to carry out a study quickly, within a matter of months rather than years, so that there is inadequate time to make baseline measurements, or where the study is regional or local rather than national in nature, since a national sample is usually too small to give precise figures for small areas. As noted above, they are also less flexible as to content, so their use for evaluation assumes that it is within a major policy domain for which standard information will serve.

A more recent development, in part an extension of the social indicators movement, is the growth in the Third World of social impact assessment (SIA). This type of study has existed in one form for some time in long-term field research in social anthropology (Foster *et al*. 1979) in studies such as those of the impact of planned resettlement (e.g. in Zambia–Colson 1960; Scudder 1962; Scudder and Colson 1979). But SIA has a different origin, in the environment movement and concern that a limited economic perspective on technological change (reflected in techniques like cost-benefit analysis) may ignore social factors and the unintended social effects of actions. Requirements in North America for environmental impact assessment (EIA) of biophysical effects led on to SIA of the demographic, social and economic aspects of planned intervention (Carley 1986). The task of SIA is to describe and analyse real or potential effects of proposed projects upon specific groups of people. Its use in development studies is yet at an early stage, but it promises to be a useful tool to add to the social indicator type inquiry (Derman and Whiteford 1985). How far it is distinctive from applied social science is debatable, but SIA does focus attention upon the immediate consequences of policy in a way that some conventional approaches do not.

Donald Warwick's study of the implementation of population policies exemplifies the use of sociological research to probe in depth the reasons for the success or failure of particular policies. As already noted, he analysed (1982, Part III) the role of officials and their ambivalence, the commitment of implementers, the role of opinion leaders and the responses of clients. He also points out, however, that programmes for population limitation are promulgated within cultures that carry distinctive attitudes to child-rearing. The cultural bias of all countries studied was toward fertility and against sterility. In Egypt, a first source of pronatalism was the expectation of universal and early marriage for women (Warwick 1982, pp. 108–10). A woman's most important functions in life are to bear children and raise a family. Women, once married, were expected in Egyptian villages to have children quickly. Augmenting these pressures in many countries is a strong preference for male children. These beliefs about marriage and reproduction are linked to beliefs that a large family is economically necessary. Particularly in rural areas, the economic value of additional children is substantial and often irreplaceable. Children also provide added security in old age, proof of parental (especially male) sexuality, or may be regarded as an expression of God's will, not subject to human intervention in the form of family planning. This is not to say that human behaviour cannot change, nor that people are not receptive to propaganda and appliances for family planning. It does, however, point to the importance of cultural context for reproductive decisions, and the high cost of ignoring those contexts in promulgating policies. Moreover, such policies and programmes cannot hope to stimulate demand for family planning when the objective and subjective interests of clients are served by large families.

Such studies are a contribution to a growing literature upon implementation of policy, to which sociologists have a significant contribution to make. So far the main running has been made by political scientists, more attuned to the political system and how policy is shaped within it (cf. Grindle 1980). Warwick's discussion of the general principles of implementation comes down in favour of a transactional model of implementation. Implementers have continually to deal with tasks, environments, clients and each other. The key to success is continual coping with contexts, personalities, alliances and events. Adaptability requires the willingness to correct mistakes, shift direction, and learn from doing. 'Nothing is more vital to implementation than self-correction; nothing more lethal than blind perseveration' (1982, p. 190). In contributing to that self-correction, sociological research has a particularly important part to play, in helping to grasp the social context of policy, the constraints which this imposes and the opportunities which it affords.

The point may be generalised to development planning by saying that sociological research provides a means of focusing upon people as participants in and clients of the development process. Technological and economic analyses can only take one so far, when social, cultural and structural factors may influence people's behaviour in ways not anticipated in technocratic models. Sociological research can provide insight into these 'people' factors, not least in evaluation studies. It is appropriate to conclude this discussion by quoting from a systematic analysis of sixty-eight evaluations of completed development projects by an American anthropologist:

Putting people first in development interventions means eliciting the needs for change that they perceive; identifying culturally compatible goals and strategies for change; developing socially appropriate, workable, and efficient designs for innovation; using, rather than opposing, existing groups and organizations; drawing on participants' informal monitoring and evaluation of projects during implementation; and gathering detailed information before and after implementation so that socioeconomic impact can be accurately assessed. These tasks are specific illustrations of the continuous need for social expertise from identification to impact evaluation (Kottak 1985, p. 326).

4 Margaret Hardiman

Sociological perspectives on w
and development policy

Sociologists have had a lot to say about women and development. Many studies have been made about the effects of socio-economic change on the position of women, and although there is always room for more research there is certainly no dearth of existing knowledge. The excellent annotated bibliography prepared by May Rihani (1978) for the Overseas Development Council is just one example of the mass of literature available, and increasingly this is being contributed to by sociologists and anthropologists from developing countries.

Although these studies have helped to reinforce the efforts of those concerned with the issues of women in development it is questionable to what extent sociologists have influenced development policies, no doubt because so little of the research undertaken has specifically addressed itself to policy questions. The issue of women is certainly given greater importance in national plans and documents (World Bank 1979), but too often this only amounts to lip-service being paid, without any real attempt to tackle the fundamental problems involved. Too often the women themselves are hardly brought into the process of decision-making; instead assumptions are made about where their interests lie and what sort of programmes are appropriate to meet their needs. In order to consider the reasons for the neglect of women in development, and the consequence of this for the whole development process, this chapter will first address the question of the case for separate consideration of women. It will then turn to the relevance of sociological research for policy and planning purposes, leading to a consideration of the policy implications of this research. Finally it will suggest strategies for making greater use of a sociological perspective in policy-making and planning.

he case for treating women separately

Women form roughly half the population of the world so it might be assumed that they have equal interests in the development of policies for their countries. In terms of interests this is indeed true, but in terms of policy formulation it is a very different matter. In many societies they tend to be overlooked, to be 'invisible' when it comes to decision-making. It is assumed that their interests are taken care of by their husbands, or fathers or brothers, or even sons. They may reign supreme in the domestic domain, but outside the household their views are ignored. So the first strong reason for taking account of women as a separate category is that due attention must be given to their views. Another reason is that women have special interests which concern them, such as maternal and child health. Fathers, it is true, are also parents and should concern themselves about these matters. But it is women who are most likely to bear the day-to-day responsibility for the rearing of children and the environmental health of the household. This reason for taking account of women is more generally recognised as it accords with her 'domestic role' image, and is often, along with handicrafts, the main focus of so-called 'women's programmes'. But in terms of allocation of funds it tends to be given low priority.

A more cogent reason for considering women relates to their economic role. Women contribute substantially to family incomes and to a greater extent than most labour statistics indicate. It is extraordinarily difficult to obtain reliable data on this subject, as Boserup (1970) found in her seminal book on *Woman's Role in Economic Development*. Since then the outpourings of international agencies have not been particularly helpful. For example, the World Bank's annual *World Development Report* makes no attempt to assess the proportion of women in the labour force, no doubt because of the unreliability of national statistics, and even the more detailed ILO statistics underestimate women's economic role.

Added to these general reasons is the anxiety that the situation of women in poor countries has deteriorated markedly in recent years. The report of the mid-decade conference of the UN Decade of Women held in Copenhagen in 1980 noted that 'In particular, it worsened with respect to the conditions of employment and education for women in the rural and so-called marginal urban sectors. In many countries the actual number of female illiterates is increasing . . . In many countries, transfer of inappropriate technology has worsened the employment and health conditions of women. In many countries women have not been integrated into national development plans.'

Although caution must be exercised over the theory of increasing misery, as sometimes it is more an increasing realisation of a long-existing situation, there are undoubtedly cases where a worsening of women's position can be documented.

Development planning has often exacerbated the situation. As Rogers (1980, p. 175) observes: 'Much development planning adversely affects women by depriving them of important resources and by intensifying their workload while reducing their control over their own work patterns.' Rogers gives many examples of how the discrimination in development projects works in practice, such as the response to a question on one of her visits: 'I've just been filling in a questionnaire from headquarters about women. But you know there's hardly anything to say, because we don't have the sort of projects that would involve them . . . you see all our projects here are concerned with cattle, and it just so happens that women have very few cattle. Of course we get criticized because cattle are owned by the richer people.' (Rogers 1980, p. 55). The omission of women is largely due to erroneous assumptions of planners, most of them men. Dulansey (1977) spells out some of these as:

(a) men are the principal labourers in society;
(b) men are the heads of households;
(c) men are the primary breadwinners, and their wages constitute family incomes;
(d) women and men have equal access to educational opportunities;
(e) women and men have equal access to credit opportunities; and
(f) women and men eat proportionate shares of the food available to the family.

In the following section of this chapter it will be shown that these assumptions by no means reflect the fully reality.

Finally, an important reason for directing special attention to women is the positive contribution they can make to development, not only in their directly economic role but more generally in terms of social development. There are clear indications that, where more women are literate and have a better status, this is reflected in more favourable social indicators such as infant mortality, life expectancy, nutritional status, and the incidence of morbidity and mortality from easily preventable diseases. The reasons outlined above for the special consideration of women in development planning are fairly obvious and uncontroversial. More contentious is the value of the sociologist's contribution, either as researcher or as consultant.

The sociologist's contribution

This question needs to be looked at from two broad points of view. Firstly, in what ways are research findings useful for policy and project planning purposes, and how can these findings be operationalised? Secondly, what role has the sociologist in the planning process? This latter question is dealt with comprehensively in other chapters and, although there are few specific references to women, the points made are equally relevant.

Research, and the debates arising out of it, have highlighted the complexity of issues relating to women and development. They need to be viewed in historical perspective and in both a national and international context, in order to arrive at an understanding of the 'deeply rooted reasons which prevent women's issues being considered an integral part of development questions' (Ahooja-Patel 1982, p. 18). This viewpoint leads to the belief that it is time to move beyond simple truisms to a deeper analysis of the mechanisms perpetuating the subordination of women. Such an analysis involves looking at systems of economic organisation and how these affect not only women but male-female relationships; in other words, it raises the whole issue of the nature of established political systems. It follows from this that prescriptions for development policies based on such research will not only take very different forms in different country situations, but will in turn be influenced by the viewpoint of the researcher.

Before looking more closely at some research findings it is important to clarify what criteria are used for measuring the position of women in society. Conventional indicators use the proportion of women to men in the labour force and the enrolment of women at different educational levels. Even when disaggregated by some definition of occupational status and earnings, labour statistics are not altogether satisfactory. Not only do they fail to record much of women's work, they also have low discriminatory meaning in some socioeconomic situations. Little has been done to measure the relationship of work with economic power and to what extent economic independence is reflected in the political and jural domains (Hardiman 1970). The question of political power is of obvious relevance to women's status; to what extent do they participate in political institutions, in what ways are they involved in pressure groups, such as trade unions? Some measurement of these aspects is available and they demonstrate more than other indicators the inequalities that exist. They do not necessarily show much positive correlation with the more conventionally used labour and educational indicators.

Throughout this research for appropriate indicators the question arises of who should make value judgements about a woman's social position. It raises cross-cultural issues and the need to distinguish between role enactment and role expectations. A great deal of research in Third World countries has been undertaken by foreigners; however good their training in research methods there is a danger of ethnocentricity, and this bias can also affect Third World sociologists who have been educated in the West and come from very different backgrounds than their respondents. 'What women do' is one matter; 'what women think they should do' is another, which is not only more difficult to assess, but even when not ignored, can so easily be distorted by the methodological approach used, the type of questions asked. Women's perception of their role is heavily influenced by the socialisation process; this does not make it less relevant as a factor to consider in formulating policies. It therefore needs to be understood and taken into consideration.

Research into women's issues is broadly of two kinds; macro-level, which addresses issues on a broad front, using comparative data; and micro-level, which concerns itself with a specific community. Macro-level studies focus on the broad socio-economic features of underdevelopment and its causes; they offer valuable insights into the differences and similarities on an international scale, but they may be difficult to apply in particular situations. Micro-level studies are highly relevant to the particular situation; their limitations lie in the extent to which lessons can be learnt that are applicable in other contexts.

Ester Boserup's book on *Woman's Role in Economic Development* (1970) is a good example of the value of macro-level studies. Although the data on which the analysis was based need to be updated, the implications of its findings are still relevant. For the first time it systematically documented the consequences of economic development for the traditional divisions of labour by sex. Boserup considered this in relation to farming systems, to commerce, trade and industry, and to the rise of the professions. She demonstrated that, in these occupations, the progress towards an increasingly intricate pattern of labour specialisation had tended to disfavour women. Take, for example, agriculture; Boserup distinguishes between 'male and female farming systems', the former characterising mainly regions of plough cultivation, the latter being found where shifting cultivation prevails. Africa is the region of female farming *par excellence* where, in many cases, most of the tasks connected with food production are performed by women. Traditionally, men were responsible for clearing the ground; they were also hunters and warriors. To what extent they took part in other farm activities varied between communities, but in general their work load was less, particularly when food storage and traditional marketing are added to the list; these two tasks almost invariably fell to women. How and why has there been a change in this pattern? One reason was the policies of colonial rulers who, accustomed to the male farming systems in their own countries, imported their ideas to Africa. They perceived the men as underemployed, often referred to them as 'lazy', and tried to induce them to take a more active part in agriculture, particularly in the cultivation of commercial crops for export. A further inducement to growing cash crops was provided by the imposition of a poll tax. Women were left in the subsistence sector of the rural economy and this was further exacerbated by the colonial rulers' recruitment of men to work in road building, mines and plantations.

This analysis is borne out by more detailed studies in Africa, such as that by Mbilinyi (1975). She uses Tanzanian women as an example to illustrate women's position over time. She maintains that pre-colonial social and economic dominance by males was enhanced during the colonial period when education and cash crop farming were made available to men, thus greatly reducing the overall importance of the female role. Muntemba (1982) shows that in Zambia today women carry the main burden of food production; this has happened both because of the intensification of cash crop production, dominated by men, and the higher rate of male migration to urban areas, notably the Copper Belt. In some rural districts in 1969 there were eighty males to one hundred females and in others thirty to fifty per cent of the households were headed by women. Muntemba attempts 'to understand the position of women as food producers and suppliers within the framework of the social relations of production, distribution and surplus appropriation' (Muntemba 1982, p. 30), and believes that by so doing it is possible to get at the fundamental cause of the problem.

She discusses the question of control over and access to land and other means of production, including the crucial factor of labour. In order for a woman to ensure non-appropriation and fair distribution she must have control over her own labour and the product of that labour. The struggle over factors of production is not a new phenomenon, but Muntemba contends that the penetration of capitalism and the money economy most markedly, and devastatingly, challenged the position of women.

Although farming systems in Asia, which are mainly based on plough cultivation, are very different from those in Africa, and women tend to have a more subordinate position in society, many similarities exist with regard to the affects of development. For example, a village study group in Bangladesh (Adnan *et al*. 1976) revealed the value of women's economic role. They worked on average ten to fourteen hours a day on seed and grain storage and preservation, post-harvest rice-processing, vegetable and fruit-growing, poultry-raising, livestock care, food-processing, household manufacture, building maintenance and repair and fuel and water-gathering. In this and another paper delivered at the same seminar in Dacca (Abdullah and Zeidenstein 1976) attention is drawn to the lack of appreciation generally given to women's contribution, leading to their neglect in policy formulation. Modernisation efforts involving traditional female activities are aimed at men so that women do not have the opportunity to acquire new skills which could raise their productivity. Purdah is often seen as an obstacle; these papers consider that it need not be a barrier to change if appropriate policies are devised, such as providing skills training at sites suitable for women, including leadership and management training. A plea is made for avoiding urban solutions to rural problems; instead programmes should build on the knowledge and expertise which women already possess.

Boserup (1970) begins her discussion of the role of women in urban development with an analysis of their role in market trade. She points to the striking differences between the roles which men and women play in trade in various parts of the world. The market women of Ghana are famous; they constitute eighty per cent of the labour force in trade, and ninety-four per cent of them are trading on their own account. By contrast very few women in regions of Arab influence are engaged in trade, although data on this may be misleading as women living in house seclusion frequently use intermediaries to trade on their behalf (Hardiman 1974). In Asia a variety of patterns is found: in Burma, Thailand, Cambodia and the Philippines women account for around fifty per cent of the total labour force in trade, whereas in India, Sri Lanka and Malaysia the rate is around ten per cent.

As most women in trade are working on their own account their turnover tends to be small, although there are instances of Ghanaian women with credits of thousands of pounds sterling with overseas firms (Boserup 1970, p. 93). Moreover, as a great deal of their trading activity is part-time, fitted in with both domestic and agricultural work, they tend to remain in the informal sector of the economy. The modern trade sector of shops and supermarkets is manned mainly by men, even in Ghana where women constitute no more than twenty-four per cent of the labour force. An exception to this is found in Latin America where the modernisation of the trade sector appears to have strengthened the female element in the labour force. This may be due to a higher level of female literacy in Latin America than in Asia or Africa; also to different cultural traditions, a higher rate of female migration to towns and a more advanced level of economic development. In all industrialised countries the proportion of women among trade employees is high at between thirty-five and fifty-five per cent.

Women are generally less well represented in modern industry than in trade, as most of those in industry are working on their own account or as part of the family labour force. Home-based industries, such as food-processing, brewing of beer, spinning and weaving, basket-making and pottery are traditional. The processes were simple and known by most men, women and children (Geertz 1963). The critical question to examine is what happens to these domestic industries when a country develops capital-intensive manufacturing industries and how does this affect women's roles? Boserup's analysis (1970, p. 111) suggests that when larger industries gradually drive the home industries out of business women lose their jobs. In all the countries for which she collected data there was a lower percentage of women among hired workers than among own-account and family workers. The reasons for this lie on both the supply and demand sides of the female labour market. Employers tend to prefer men, and this is often reinforced by legislation which enforces obligatory benefits to women workers such as maternity leave and crèches, or prohibition of work on night shifts. But often the women themselves prefer to work at home, and in many societies this is more socially acceptable. Not only are working hours more flexible, but the risk of exploitation and male harassment is avoided. Factory work by women is frowned on in most Third World countries notably in the Arab world. As women tend to hold the worst paid and often most precarious jobs in modern industry their presence in the labour force is unlikely to enhance their status. An alternative, more appropriate to the Third World type of industrialisation, is needed to improve the lot of both men and women in the industrial labour force (Steady 1982). The record of industrialised countries shows that increased participation does not automatically lead to a reduction of the male/female wage earnings gap, or an improvement in the status of women. Even such interventions as the Equal Opportunities Commission or Equal Pay Act in Britain have not proved of much benefit to women. In some ways these measures seem to have increased segregation and wage disadvantage (Young and Smith 1983). Between 1911 and 1971 women's share of skilled manual work dropped from 24% to 13.5%, and over the same period their share of unskilled manual jobs rose from 15.6% to 37.2%.

In modern sector occupations requiring education women are at a disadvantage in most countries because of their disadvantage in access to educational opportunities. This is universally true in Africa, and Asia, with the exception of the Philippines and Hong Kong; in Latin America women are well represented in the education system at all stages, including higher education, and this is reflected in their representation in professional occupations, which in some Latin American countries is fifty per cent or more. But even here they are unlikely to be found in large numbers in the higher echelons of their profession. The importance of education to women's position is universally recognised, but although there has been an undoubted change in attitudes in recent years, sociological research indicates the difficulties inherent in radically altering the situation. Even in developed countries, where, in theory, boys and girls enjoy the same educational opportunities, there seem to be subtle factors working against the interests of women.

Surveys in Britain have shown that 'the majority of teachers state that they are opposed to sexual discrimination and that they personally do not discriminate but treat students equally and fairly' (Young and Smith 1982, p. 91). Yet the drop-out rate for girls after the compulsory school-leaving age continues to be greater, fewer continue to A-level, and only thirty-five per cent of undergraduates are women. Moreover, they tend to specialise, both at school and university in subjects which are generally regarded as suitable for women, and are poorly represented in engineering and technology (there are less than five per cent of women undergraduates in these fields) and science (under one third of women undergraduates). Only twenty-six per cent of post graduates in Britain are women and the proportion of women academic staff in Universities is even less at around fifteen per cent. So the problem is deeply-rooted in British society, involving attitudes to women which are slow to change. They are still encouraged to think of themselves more as wives and mothers than as active participants in the labour force. The hidden curriculum makes its indelible mark at an early age, leading to too many girls leaving school without useful skills, and thinking of work rather in terms of 'jobs' than 'careers'. If a woman wakes up to her lack of education later in life what chances has she to make up for her deficiencies? Opportunities for continuing education have certainly improved and many late starters have benefited from such facilities as the Open University and the polytechnics. Unfortunately recent Government cuts will jeopardise these facilities and women will be among the chief losers.

Returning to this issue in the Third World, many of the same factors operate. Girls tend to be channelled into 'women's subjects' and the professions most suited to them are thought of as teaching, nursing and social work. The case of Latin America has already been cited, where women are well represented both in higher education and in the professions. But here again the majority of them are in teaching or nursing. In Africa and Asia the proportion of women in the professions is lower, except in the Philippines where it is similar to Latin America, a reflection of the larger proportion of women in higher education. In the Philippines however, the same pattern of occupations prevails; nearly seventy per cent of nurses are women and nearly eighty per cent of teachers. It is significant that, despite their predominance in the teaching profession, they tend to be in primary rather than secondary schools, and disproportionately few are principals.

These, then, are just some of the findings of sociological research that throw light on the position of women, and the likely effects that socio-economic change may have on them. Sociological studies challenge many common assumptions, not least on the effects of 'modernisation' on family organisation. For example, Oppong's (1976) study of Ghanaian women teachers considers two assumptions commonly found in the literature on family change: '1) that 'modernisation', including migration, industrialisation, urbanisation and education, will break down traditional extended family organisation and lead to 'modern' conjugal family systems, and 2) that women benefit from these changes by attaining increased equality with their husbands, individual autonomy and freedom from familial constraints' (Oppong 1976, p. 6). This study is a good example of in-depth research, using the methodology of social anthropology, to look at the jointness/segregation of the husband-wife relationship in the context of 'extended', 'joint' or 'nuclear' families. One important finding is that the concept of the 'extended family' is an ideal type, seldom matched by reality, but often used by policy-makers with regard to such decisions as how to provide child care. Many of the female Ghanaian primary school teachers were found to head their own families with no outside assistance, and two-thirds of the couples reported child-care as a problem when both parents worked.

This account of some sociological research shows that there is already a great deal of material available for policy-makers to take into account in planning projects and programmes. There is still, however, need for further specialised research. On the one hand more detailed information is needed at grass roots level in relation to specific areas and projects. Much of this research need not be academically sophisticated, and can often be undertaken more effectively by local people who will themselves be involved in the project. Such strategies will be further discussed in the following section. The other specialist need is for research into policy-making. How and by whom are policies formulated? What criteria are taken into account? What are the outcomes of these policies in their effects on women? What factors lead to the success or failure of programmes specifically directed towards women? Sociologists and social anthropologists have been slow to take up these problems; too often they have been looked on as 'applied' research, in some sense inferior to so-called 'pure' research because of the normative concepts involved (Robertson 1984).

Policy implications of the sociological perspective

The sociological perspective is essentially a method of looking at situations which takes account of the ways in which the political, economic and social dimensions of society affect people's lives. If it is to inform planners and policy-makers it must be able to afford insights into the affects of alternative development strategies. What then can

our present state of knowledge tell us about the impact of development policies on women, and can it offer guidelines for the formulation of policies, projects and programmes in the future?

The findings outlined in the previous section enable some general
points to be made. For example, it has been seen that the majority of
women have little control over the instruments of economic and
political power. It follows that decisions about women's role in
development are mainly taken by men. The underlying problems
have in consequence often been ignored, such as the relevance of land
ownership in communities where women make a major contribution
to agricultural production. Until more recognition is given to the
interests of women and their rights to participate in decision-making a
major reversal of the status quo is unlikely. Ultimately this is a
political issue which underlies all the implications treated in this
section; the extent to which measures will be effective will depend on
the political commitment of those concerned. But, in the meantime,
what can be done to improve decision-making in the absence of
fundamental structural changes which would strengthen the position
of women in the political domain?

In the first instance research can inform the questions that policy-
makers should ask in formulating their programmes. As an example,
the recent Oxfam Field Directors' Handbook (Oxfam 1985), which
pays far greater attention to women in development than any previous
handbook, suggests a checklist of questions to be asked in assessing a
project:

1. How does the project affect the division of labour and the use of women's
   time and labour?
2. How does it affect the distribution of resources within the domestic
   economy and community between men and women?
3. What provision is there for specialised health care for women, especially
   those pregnant and mothers of young children?
4. Is there provision for educational programmes for women (literacy,
   marketable vocational training, etc)?
5. Are economic programmes merely adding to the work of women without
   really adding to their disposable income?
6 What child care is available for working women? (Oxfam 1985, p. 70).

The ability to answer these questions depends on a thorough knowledge of the community. It implies that generalisations at a national,
or a regional, level or assumptions about women's role, cannot be
taken for granted. Assumptions that women are rarely household

heads, or major contributors to household income, are common. The reality of the situation needs to be investigated, and this investigation must include the views of women themselves; too often the opinions of men in the community are taken as representing what women think. A very different point of view may emerge if instead the women are consulted, as was the case in Maiduguri (Hardiman 1974) on the question of secondary occupation.

It may be objected that policy-makers cannot wait for the results of in-depth research and that such research is expensive. The question of timing certainly does present difficulties, but it is often better to delay a project. For example, in a national project in Bangladesh to find ways expense is concerned, there are low-cost methods which have not only proved reliable, but have been of long-term benefit to the objectives of a project. For example in a national project in Bangladesh to find ways of integrating women into the development process the lack of accurate information about rural women's life and work led to the need to collect relevant data (Abdullah and Zeidenstein 1976). A number of reasons were suggested for this lack of information: the social invisibility of women, a lack of motivation on the part of researchers into rural problems to learn about women, and the lack of a conceptual framework for looking at women as a separate sub-culture. Some of the attitudes and obstacles to initiating development programmes for women are based on a lack of appreciation for what they already contribute to the economy, as has been mentioned previously in relation to the tendency to direct modernisation efforts to men. Abdullah and Zeidenstein decided to train local women ('barefoot sociologists') to interview and collect accurate, objective data. They reckoned that using such research assistants would be much more likely to reveal the true dimensions of women's role; and this they found to be so. My own experience bears out the advantages of using local people as research assistants if they are properly trained (Hardiman 1977). Quite apart from their greater knowledge of the community, they are far less likely than university students to make up answers to questions, and their enthusiasm for the task is a great source of strength.

The use of 'barefoot sociologists' also serves an educational purpose, as is shown by the methods of data collection used in the Serabu Hospital Village Health Project in Sierra Leone (Hardiman 1986). This was a small-scale project aimed at improving the health of village people. Before deciding what steps should be taken a survey was carried out in seven villages in order to assess the problems, the village people themselves helping to collect the data. As a result they gained insight into the nature and causes of morbidity and mortality and were quick to share these insights with the community at large. This led to responses, with suggestions as to how problems could be overcome. A striking example was the response of the women's 'Bundu Sande' (the women's 'secret' society) when they learnt of the incidence of neo-natal tetanus and its causes. They suggested that tetanus immunisation should be included in the puberty rites of girls and this was duly implemented. Within a short time no deaths from neo-natal tetanus were recorded in the project villages. This example has many lessons for policy-makers, not least the great potential for development that exists within communities if only it can be harnessed (Hardiman 1984b). Policy-makers not only need to know about the existing situation, they need to pay much more attention than hitherto to consulting *all* the people, including women, and involving them as closely as possible in the decision-making process (Midgley *et al.* 1986).

Having studied the situation, having consulted the women themselves to assess their perception of needs, can experience throw any light on measures which have proved successful in improving women's position and their contribution to development? As mentioned above, insufficient research on these matters has been done, but by looking more closely at specific instances some guidelines can be suggested. Devaki Jain's (1980) account of five Indian case studies is valuable because she deliberately used a sociological approach in her study. She chose five projects which claimed to have reached poor women, and where women were active participants in the organisations. As she had a very low budget the household surveys she made had to be informal and could only 'provide a glimpse into the women's perception of their participation, some insights into the kind of impact the project had on their economic and social condition – but not of the quality or size that could be termed impact studies' (Jain 1980, p. 4). In some cases she was able to use investigations by other people or organisations, but in general there was no satisfactory baseline data. Nevertheless she was able to draw some important lessons from the studies, at least as far as the position of women in India is concerned. Before looking at these lessons two of the cases will be briefly described. One is the Self-Employed Women's Association (SEWA), registered as a trade union in the city of Ahmedabad, the other is the role of women in the Anand Milk Producers' Union Ltd (AMUL) of the Kaira district of Gujarat.

SEWA was born in 1972 as an offshoot of the long-established Textile Labour Assocation which had been founded in 1917 by Mahatma Gandhi for workers in the textile mills of Ahmedabad. An interesting, if unusual, feature of this trade union was that its first president was a woman, Anasuyaben, sister of the prominent textile owner, Ambalal Sarabhai. She attended the London School of Economics from 1911—13 and on her return to Ahmedabad dedicated her life to the service of workers and their families. In 1954 the TLA created a women's wing and it was to this organisation that a forty-strong group of women headloaders came in late 1971 to complain about their wages. Their protests were followed by grievances from hand-cart pullers and used garment workers, and this led to the decision of the women to set up a new association of their own. In so doing they were greatly assisted by the staff of the women's wing of TLA, who not only moved over to work for SEWA, but provided office space without rental and an initial loan of Rs. 5,000. In April 1972 SEWA registered as a trade union, and this legal basis of their position is an important strength. The founder members were soon joined by other women working in the informal sector, such as vegetable vendors, milkmaids, carpenters, smiths, bidi workers, pappad makers and agricultural labourers. The SEWA staff held meetings to discover the needs of these women and this was followed by detailed surveys. This emphasis on thorough detailed research, sympathetically studying the problems, is central to SEWA and is an ongoing task of their field workers. The surveys undertaken revealed the extent of exploitation, economic distress, overwork, and ill health suffered by the women. The main trouble-prone areas in their lives were lack of capital, harassment from the municipal authorities and the police, and poverty-induced family problems.

SEWA's policies were based on these findings. One of the most important practical steps developed was to make capital available, which in the first instance was achieved through SEWA acting as an intermediary with the banks and later by setting up their own bank, the Mahila SEWA Sahakari Bank. Another development was to provide legal support for individuals against the authorities, or exploitative private entrepreneurs. The problems of poverty were addressed in 1975 by the setting up of the Mahila SEWA Trust to provide maternity, widowhood and death assistance schemes for members.

The Trust has also started day care centres, kindergarten and elementary classes, functional literacy classes and occupational training courses.

SEWA has become widely acclaimed as a success story, so what lessons can be learnt from its mode of operation? Has it developed a methodology for helping poor women, and tackling the hard-to-overcome problems that challenge development, that can be replicated elsewhere? The first lesson is one that has already been emphasised repeatedly in this chapter, that is, the importance of a detailed study of the problems. Another condition of success stressed by the organisers of SEWA is the need for women to have their own organisation over which they exercise control. Women are economic agents whose work and income is as vital to society as their home-bound life, but this is rarely sufficiently recognised by men. Women therefore need to be independent and self-reliant, liberated from their ingrained self-image as weak and helpless. SEWA added to this the Gandhian values of honesty, dignity and simplicity of life as guiding principles. It follows from this that education and training are an essential part of the programme if women are to learn to handle their own affairs. The socio-economic surveys of SEWA revealed that between eighty and ninety per cent of the 10,000 or so women members were illiterate, and very few had had any training in their trades.

Another lesson is the importance of a well-run, efficient organisation. SEWA has laid down procedures for the payment of membership dues, for grouping according to trades and geographical locations, for the appointment and training of group leaders, for the Representative Council and so forth. The role of the General Secretary, Mrs Ela Bhatt, a founder member, who was also chief of the women's wing of TLA, and her staff is crucial. These women are well-educated, come mainly from middle-class backgrounds, and are responsible for running the office and undertaking the fieldwork. They spend a great deal of time in the field, resolving members' trade-related problems, giving advice on personal matters, teaching women about saving, cleanliness, children's education, addressing and managing meetings, and so on. They are central to the principle of mobilisation which is the fulcrum of SEWA's operations.

The case of the Anand Milk Producers' Union Ltd (AMUL) is very different from SEWA. It was neither founded by women, nor were its objectives particularly focused on women. It could be taken as an example of a programme which was formulated without taking account of women's point of view. It assumed that women would benefit from a general improvement in family income and the 'trickle-down effect' of more prosperous villages which could afford better amenities. But AMUL is of particular interest to policy-makers in that dairying is one of the more popular support programmes for rural women, who traditionally are associated with animal husbandry. Moreover AMUL has received worldwide acclaim as a successful example of the benefits of co-operative organisation. Before considering in what way AMUL has affected women's development a brief account will be given of its operation. AMUL's beginnings lay in the formation of the first primary-level co-operative in 1946, which was founded to protect the small dairy farmers of Kaira district from the low and fluctuating prices they were receiving for their milk from middlemen. By 1948 there were eight village co-operatives; they formed a new union of milk producers which collected and pasteurised about 5,000 litres a day at a central dairy in Anand for despatch to the Bombay Milk Scheme. From these small beginnings AMUL has grown into an organisation with over 2,000 salaried employees at headquarters and 6,000 employees at the primary co-operative level; it owns a modern dairy which not only receives, processes and distributes milk, but manufactures butter, cheese, milk powder and other dairy products; it has developed a package of services to raise the productivity of milch animals, such as veterinary care (over fifty vets are employed), improved cattle-feed and better breeding stock.

The AMUL system is based on certain values and techniques. It has a rural bias, expressed in the belief in taking services to the peasantry, faith in the peasants' ability to manage, and faith in the co-operative as a form of organisation. Its methodology is to have a single entry point, milk, and the back-up services connected with milk yields; in this it differs from projects advocating an integrated approach to rural development. The main initial task, therefore, was to build up a system of collection and sale of milk, including a guarantee to members to buy all the milk they offered for sale. This was done by organising twice daily collections from all the villages in the union, and making immediate cash payments to members. The communication system built up in this way is an impressive feature. It has yielded the additional benefit of providing a daily link for village people with the outside world, a link which is heavily used for transmission of messages about sick animals, shortages of fodder, calling of meetings and so forth. Most Indian villages suffer from poor communication and very few 'extension' services reach them. In Kaira district this is no longer so true as a result of AMUL.

In 1978 a sample survey was made by an all-woman team of six, including one sociologist, to assess the impact of AMUL on women. Only about ten per cent of AMUL members are women, although they are the main controllers of dairying operations in the household. The survey collected a lot of data about households, the sample being stratified in order to represent different asset categories, based on the extent of ownership of animals and land. The respondents were women, and as well as obtaining background data about caste, family size, sex ratios, marital status, education, work-participation rates, occupation, income and expenditure, indebtedness and co-operative membership, questions were asked about the women's perceptions of the impact and main benefits of AMUL and the attitude of co-operative staff to women members. Most of the women agreed that family income had increased as a result of the co-operative, although in this, as with other indicators, it was the women from richer families who noted the biggest increase (eighty-four per cent of those in households with over five acres of land and buffaloes, against only fifty-nine per cent of those with buffaloes but no land). Health care was reckoned to have improved, as had the availability of clothing to the household, although the respondents themselves seem to have benefited less than other members. School attendance had improved; again there was a considerable difference between the richer households, and also for the poorer groups between boys and girls. Asked about the improvement of treatment by husbands seventy-four per cent of the richer respondents recorded better treatment against only twenty-one per cent of the poorer group. Likewise, seventy-one per cent of the richer women thought their status in the house had been enhanced, compared with twenty-eight per cent of the poorer respondents. So AMUL may be said to have made some positive contribution to development for women.

But the negative aspects of the findings are also significant. The attitude of AMUL co-operative staff to women seeking enrolment was consistently reported as hostile. Women were not invited to meetings, they were not treated as equal to men, and they were ignored by extension services. It was never suggested that they might occupy salaried positions in the village co-operatives where, in all cases, it was men who received, tested and gave payment for milk, and they were hardly represented at all at headquarters. The only exception to this was in one village where the co-operative was started by a remarkable woman, and run entirely by women. Her experience showed her that men were no better than women in managing public affairs. As a member of the local *panchayat* she found men ignorant, petty and incompetent, qualities that men usually attribute to women. However her views on women were also depressing. She did not find it difficult to get them to join the co-operative, but she found them not really interested in running it, nor unduly concerned about their lack of independence; the survival of the co-operative seemed to depend too much on her own presence. These attitudes and images take time to change, longer in the atmosphere of the village than in the bustling streets of Ahmedabad.

AMUL's response to the women's issue is that it could not take on two tasks at once – bypassing the entrenched interests of middlemen and women. To achieve the first task it needed the social support of the farmers; to try to involve women at this stage would have slowed, if not killed, the enterprise. This is perhaps typical of a top-down, technocratic approach and, although AMUL started small, it has now acquired the scale of an organisation which exercises a new form of dominance. As far as women are concerned they are the main workers/producers, but in most cases they neither own the means of production nor are they members of the decision-making bodies. When interviewed they expressed dissatisfaction with, for example, the decisions about the sale price of milk. They would not have agreed to so much being withheld for profits and dividends, most of which went to the bigger shareholders; and in any case to their husbands, not themselves.

As a result of the findings from these and other cases Jain (1980) suggests that policies for women's development need to go beyond efforts to increase their income-earning abilities. Income is necessary, but not a sufficient condition for improved status either within the household or in the perception of society. She suggests that one of the levers to this improved status is the strength women gain through participation in a non-family association. Whether this association must necessarily be exclusively female is a moot point and raises issues of the class/sex analysis of inequality. In most societies, however, the reality of the situation is that women tend to be subordinated unless they have a firm control of the organisation, and this is strikingly brought out by the contrast between the experiences of SEWA and AMUL. Jain warns against the possibility of replication. But successful projects can serve as laboratories for social scientists who want to examine the effectiveness of certain systems. Unfortunately too little systematic research has been done along these lines.

Strategies making greater use of a sociological perspective

Central to the theme of this chapter is the view that a sociological perspective is an essential part of the formulation of development policies, and that this is particularly true in the case of women. If this is so then a necessary adjunct to this is that sociologists should have a bigger role in development planning. This is now more generally recognised, but their contribution is still relatively small, perhaps because there is a lack of clear understanding as to what they should be doing. This chapter has illustrated the insights that can be gained through a sociological approach, and suggested ways in which the use of this approach could be strengthened. The concluding section turns to the question of strategies.

Better-focused research has already been discussed. Institutions and individuals need to be encouraged to undertake research which addresses itself to social problems and policies. As Bulmer shows in Chapter Three, sociologists can play a vital role in gathering data for policy-makers. Governments and international agencies could commission research on a bigger scale. Good examples of such research already exist, such as Gill Shepherd's study for Oxfam of the potential for family planning programmes in Kenya (Shepherd 1984). There is no lack of scholars willing and able to carry out assessments if funds are available. Although research may be expensive it can be extremely cost-effective if it avoids wasteful and useless expenditure. The development field is already strewn with disastrous examples of mis-guided projects. Moreover, low-cost research techniques, making use of local personnel could be used to a much greater extent, and such techniques are particularly relevant to involving women. Using them as interviewers and respondents helps to awaken their consciousness, helps them to understand the causes of their problems and think of ways by which they might be overcome.

The next requirement is to employ more men and women with a sociological background in every stage of the planning process, in Central Government Planning Offices, in sectoral planning units and at regional or district level. For these people to be effective they need an education which goes beyond a single subject discipline such as sociology or social anthropology. They must develop a multi-disciplinary approach in order to communicate with colleagues and understand the working of bureaucracies. They must learn to apply knowledge in order to formulate policies (Hardiman and Midgley 1980). This last task is the one that has often caused concern amongst academics; they fear having to make recommendations at a stage when they feel they could be reserving judgement. As Midgley notes in the first chapter, they question the normative nature that is an inevitable part of decision-making. Up to a point they can present their agencies with information on the likely effects of alternative strategies. But they will lose confidence if they are never prepared to be more positive in their recommendations. Yet, as Hall shows in Chapter Two of this volume when discussing sociologists' roles within international aid organisations, there are fundamental bureaucratic and political obstacles to their greater involvement in policy formulation and project implementation.

The last paragraph referred to 'more men and women'. A better balance between the sexes is one of the important strategies to be adopted, and not only as far as the women's issue is concerned. Too often women are hired in order to plan for and work with women, and the areas in which they are expected to operate are seen as domestic concerns and subsidiary occupations such as handicrafts. In many societies the cultural setting makes it necessary to have women field workers, but their role should never be confined solely to women's affairs. As far as men are concerned they also should be aware of the existing situation of women in their society and their potential contribution to development. Ignorance is often more of a hindrance than malice and this at least can be remedied.

The sociological package is now a requirement in many foreign aid-funded consultancy assignments, but it tends to be too little and too late to have a significant impact on project design or implementation (as Hall demonstrates in Chapter Two). All that needs to be added here is to draw attention to the sex balance in consultancies, and also to recommend that more use is made of local personnel in the planning and running of projects (Hardiman and Midgley 1978). Moreover, in all projects, not only those specifically mentioning women, the women's role and point of view needs to be taken into account. Even apparently obvious matters, such as the division of labour between the sexes is too often overlooked. Women's movements throughout the world are pressing for more serious attention to the consequences for women of development policies. Many of those undertaking research are deeply committed to the women's movement (*Development Dialogue* 1982). Unfortunately their deliberations are often not taken seriously by the many men and women who are fearful of 'feminism'. It will be tragic if this attitude obscures the real need for a truly sociological perspective on women's role in development.

Community participation and development policy: a sociological perspective

Few concepts in the field of development policy-making have been as widely-used – and misused – as that of 'participation'. While the practice of active involvement by people in designing and implementing measures to improve their own welfare has existed throughout recorded history, only recently, within the last fifteen years or so, has the concept become part of the international language of development institutions. The large and ever-expanding volume of literature on the subject reflects the fact that, for many theoreticians and practitioners of development, 'participation' has become an article of faith, a fundamental prerequisite for any successful project or programme, and the single most important key to improving the livelihoods of the world's poor. Yet systematic analysis of the origins and application of this concept makes it apparent that 'participation' has many different interpretations, and that it has frequently been used to manipulate the beneficiaries of development initiatives rather than allow them greater control over directed socio-economic changes affecting their lives.

The idea of participation as a basic ingredient for assisting progress, particularly in the rural sector, sprang to a large degree from disillusionment with growth strategies imported into the developing world from the West during the 1950s and 60s. These stressed capital-intensive industrialisation, the rapid commercialisation of agriculture, heavy infrastructural investments and the transformation of traditional values as the appropriate strategy for achieving self-sustaining economic growth whose benefits would automatically 'trickle down' to the masses (Rosenstein-Rodan 1943; Lewis 1955; Rostow 1960). The resulting inequities and relative failure of the free market capitalist system to significantly alleviate either absolute or relative poverty levels led to a greater involvement of the State in directing resources to the needier sectors, assisted by increasingly active bilateral and multilateral aid organisations.

Thus it has been possible to observe the evolution of aid strategies which have, to varying degrees, stressed redistributive measures associated with the concept of people's participation. Although not necessarily labelled 'participation' as such, beneficiary involvement of one form or another in different stages of the project cycle has been advocated by all the major post-war development policies, including community development, *animation rurale* and the co-operative movement. The major UN agencies have all embraced participation, including the ILO, FAO, WHO, UNESCO and IFAD. The ILO developed the 'basic human needs' approach (BHN) and launched its PORP (Participatory Organisations of the Rural Poor) programme in 1977. The crucial role of participation in BHN strategy and in State-directed redistributive policies was stressed by Streeten (1981). The FAO has initiated the People's Participation Programme (PPP), while IFAD has stressed its importance in rural credit schemes (IFAD 1983). Another UN body, UNRISD, set up a major research programme into the notion and practice of participation (Pearse and Stiefel 1981).

Although many international organisations have attempted to develop a pragmatic concept of participation as a central tenet of their philosophy and activities, it must be said that much writing verges on the utopian. Gran (1983), for example, advocates a laudable if unlikely change in development strategies to emphasise 'development by people' rather than by elites. Haque *et al.* (1977) put forward the concept of 'another development' which stressed the humanistic values of 'collective creativity' and other non-quantifiable dimensions of development, aiming at a closing of the 'consciousness gap' between the leaders of society and the masses. Others adopt a rather more down-to-earth approach and see participation as instrumental in achieving material objectives. Rondinelli (1983), for example, attributes the failure of many UNDP schemes during the 1970s to a lack of popular participation by beneficiaries in implementation and evaluation. Put another way, 'a consensus has evolved that participation is a necessary condition for . . . people to manage their affairs, control their environment and enhance their own well-being' (Gow and VanSant 1983, p. 427).

An operational definition

This contrast between the pragmatic and the more philosophical views of participation makes it fairly apparent that the concept is a multi-faceted one which has been given different meanings over time. If, on the face of it, 'participation' is a conveniently neutral catch-phrase which can be incorporated into all political ideologies, its underlying assumptions must be made explicit if the term is to have any real significance. For analytical purposes, a broad distinction may be drawn between four major modes of people's participation within the context of guided social and economic change: anti-participatory, manipulative, incremental and participatory (Midgley *et al.* 1986). The anti-participatory mode precludes any form of people's involvement, while the manipulative kind is carefully planned to control popular participation entirely for the ulterior motives of serving government economic and political objectives. The incremental type is unplanned and haphazard, is implemented on an *ad hoc* basis and is commonly the result either of ambivalence towards the feasibility of popular participation or simply of inefficient planning. In the participatory mode the State makes a genuine attempt to promote people's participation, devolving decision-making power to local institutions as a corollary of basic social and economic reforms.

The first type, the anti-participatory mode, is appropriate to describe a number of regimes in the developing world in which there are no efforts whatsoever to mobilise the masses for participation, and in which the accumulation of wealth and concentration of power in the hands of the ruling class are the prime objectives of the State. Development projects in Haiti under the Duvaliers and in pre-Sandinista Nicaragua, for example, have involved no effective participation but have served principally as a means of attracting foreign exchange into government coffers and unashamedly enriching the elite.

Most development activities in the Third World, in both socialist and non-socialist blocs, fall within the manipulative and incremental categories. Yet the notion of State-directed participatory development is to a large extent self-contradictory, since any type of official involvement is bound to mean some form of control. This might signify subjecting people to crude 'top-down' planning and resource transfer along with the co-opting of potentially autonomous local movements, or a more subtle form of *laissez-faire* incrementalism which fails to support community initiatives for reasons of administrative inefficiency or political indecision. The majority of participatory programmes seem to be motivated by instrumental goals such as taking advantage of local resources or knowledge in order to reduce costs of administration and implementation, or that of increasing political support for the government.

Thus, a statist strategy of participation is based on the assumption that there exists a consensus of interests between government and most sectors of the populace and that the only acceptable situation is one of collaboration by the community with official policy. Involvement of the people is sought, but only after the major development parameters have been set by the government and the role of each group carefully prescribed. Participation is therefore conceived as another kind of resource injection from outside, necessary in order to make development activities function with as few hitches as possible. It is considered as essentially a manageable input under the control of government officials and confined to the implementation and evaluation stages of the project cycle rather than the selection or design phases.

In this sense participation is considered 'a voluntary contribution by the people to one or another of the public programmes supposed to contribute to national development but the people are not expected to take part in shaping the programme or criticising its content' (Oakley and Marsden 1984, p. 19). In other words, 'Participation seems to mean getting people to do what outsiders think is good for them' (Heyer *et al.* 1981, p. 5.). Any form of State-initiated participation is bound to be characterised by such instrumental and essentially patronising views of the participatory process, principally because a government pushing for rapid development believes it cannot afford the internal dissent and conflict which is the almost inevitable result, albeit possibly temporary, of authentic participation.

In its purest sense, authentic participation implies the involvement of a broad spectrum of the community in all phases of development activities from project selection and design through to execution and ex-post evaluation. This does not mean that people simply comply with orders from central government but that they have a certain autonomy of decision-making to actively take initiatives in this process. The central issue, then, is that of power. Communities must have some control over resources, a degree of countervailing power against that of the State. In the words of Pearse and Stiefel (1981, p.

13), '. . . the struggle for people's participation implies an attempted redistribution of both control of resources and power in favour of those who live by their own product labour.'

It is claimed by some writers that such participation in decision-making, while a central issue, is not the only dimension. Uphoff asserts, for example, that participation in benefits, implementation and evaluation are other valid forms which must be considered (Uphoff 1985). Yet experience has shown that governments do not easily make such concessions and there are, in fact, very few examples of people becoming effectively involved in planning development. Pearse and Stiefel observe that, '. . . in spite of insistence on popular participation in United Nations Development programmes, an examination of their performance is not encouraging . . . authentic popular participation seldom occurs' (quoted in Oakley and Marsden 1984, p. 29). Poor groups must, in order to have an effective voice in policy-making, have some form of bargaining power to oblige governments to take their demands seriously. This may occur through political parties, through trade unions, co-operative movements or well-organised and co-ordinated community organisations. In the truest sense of the word, therefore, participation involves 'empowerment' of the poor so that they may exert their own influence, independently of government direction, on decision-making and related activities of development projects.

Constraints on participation

Clearly, there are many obstacles to achieving participation, of whichever category. The sort of obstacles identified will tend to reflect the particular conception of participatory development being employed. These constraints may be classified into three major groups, operational, cultural and structural (Oakley and Marsden 1984, pp. 30–1). Those who see participation simply as a means of making projects run more smoothly along pre-established lines view operational problems as being of most importance. Factors such as over-centralised planning, poor delivery of services, lack of effective co-ordination, inappropriate technology and macro-economic government policies are seen as major obstacles in what is essentially a mechanistic or instrumentalist perception of participation (Uphoff 1985). Conversely, proponents of the more radical view that genuine participation should entail a sharing of power and decision-making, emphasise the socio-political or structural constraints at local, national and international levels. These include inegalitarian systems of land ownership and authority, the local and national class structure and the elitist values which perpetuate gross inequalities.

Cultural obstacles are highlighted by both schools of thought; the instrumentalist view is that traditional values are barriers to development which must be broken down to make way for more 'modern' ways of thinking, while the more radical perception of participation sees non-response by the poor as a rational reaction to official policies which are against their own best interests. In practice, of course, these three sets of factors are closely linked, so that operational and cultural considerations are bound up with the social and political structures within which development takes place. It is a moot point whether it is possible to achieve a substantial degree of community participation in the decision-making process without simultaneously undertaking structural reforms. In purely pragmatic terms, however, and in the absence of sufficiently drastic political change, one is bound to take a closer look at those operational and structural features of the planning process which work against the greater involvement of beneficiaries.

Planning for development, whether undertaken by national governments or international aid organisations, has been overwhelmingly a 'top-down' process characterised by the 'blueprint' approach; that is, the imposition of preconceived packages based to a large extent on Western experience. Policy-making has been technocratic, dominated by economists to the almost total exclusion of other social scientists, such as sociologists and anthropologists, who are more sensitive to the social or human aspects of the development process (see Hall's Chapter Two in this volume). In the rural sector policies have been based on farm management and free market ideas drawn from the West. These have emphasised capital-intensive technologies for so-called 'progressive' farmers while ignoring the majority of smallholders, landless and near-landless poor. The polarising impact of the Green Revolution has, for example, been well-documented (Griffin 1974; Pearse 1980).

Only with the advent of the World Bank's 'poverty-oriented' approach in the mid-1970s have steps been taken to redress this imbalance, although rather late in the day. The use of systems management by governments of developing countries has reinforced the trend towards centralised planning, along with the paternalistic attitudes of planners themselves, who have not considered beneficiary participation to be necessary (Rondinelli 1983). Gran (1983, p. 235) concludes that 'Projects appear almost always to have originated to fulfil the purposes of regional or national elites.' A pertinent case is that of Indonesia, where planning has been heavily top-down and officials 'overlook the fact that highly centralised control exerted by the government . . . has eroded the traditional village institutions that should support and promote rural development' (Hardjono 1983, p. 60).

Rural development, participation and the State

Although few governments have been so despotic as to allow no form of people's participation whatsoever, that which has taken place has generally been of the manipulative and instrumental kind. The reason behind the failure of the State to promote authentic participation lies in the fact that to do so is to forfeit control of national destiny. What remains, therefore, is a rather diluted form of participation which is useful to the State for achieving predetermined development goals in so far as people's involvement in programme implementation increases the efficiency of execution, and in so far as the sharing of benefits may assist economic recovery and/or political mobilisation. Participation is utilised only as long as it serves immediate official economic and political aims; it is not in any sense valued as an end in itself.

The field of rural development offers many examples of how the State has attempted to promote popular participation. Major government-directed attempts to encourage collective co-operation among rural dwellers are the community development, *animation rurale* and co-operative movements. Community development and *animation rurale*, developed initially by the British and French respectively to assist in post-independence nation-building, became very popular during the 1950s and 60s. The idea spread rapidly from Africa and the Indian sub-continent to Latin America and other parts of Asia since it appeared to offer a politically neutral mechanism for promoting economic recovery and for gaining the support of the masses. Based on the assumption of a consensus of interests between villagers and governments, as well as among the various social strata and groups in the countryside, community development workers were expected to 'awaken' the peasantry from its supposed apathy and conservatism into a new age of economic progress. The strategy was taken up by many countries, both socialist and non-socialist. In the latter group community development has been a relative failure and all but abandoned, although certain features have been retained under different labels, as in the cases of India and Mexico. Socialist States still cling to participatory ideals for the purposes of assisting in the execution of rural programmes and of political mobilisation. China, Tanzania and Ethiopia fall into this category.

The record of community development shows clearly how limited is the concept of participation employed by the State, of whatever political ideology. In spite of the rhetoric frequently employed, this philosophy became merely another mechanism for promoting existing official programmes, denying participants any real involvement in implementation. Pressures from central government 'transformed the village-level worker from a coordinator into a salesman for line ministry programmes' (Gow and VanSant 1983, p. 429). The strong social divisions within communities were generally underestimated, making the notion of collaboration spurious and the practical problems of achieving such a goal almost insurmountable. The pressure to obtain quick results led village workers and officials to rely on local elites, leading to unequal distribution of benefits and, if anything, a worsening of conflict in the countryside.

India's community development programme, with its emphasis on public works, gave 'no collective voice to exert pressure on the rest of society to give them due opportunities for growth . . . (but) . . . encouraged the process of atomisation and discouraged the formation of people's organisations' (Gaikwad 1981, p. 331). In post-revolutionary Mexico, although the one-party State does not have a single, unified community development programme, official incentives in this sphere based on the incremental model have been increasingly challenged. According to one observer such schemes 'are seen as a means of imposing the values and way of life of the promoters on others . . . designed to buy off discontent with concessions which do not tackle the underlying causes of backwardness and poverty' (Cosio 1981, p. 350).

Scepticism towards the feasibility of authentic participation under State auspices is not confined to capitalist countries. In socialist nations also, participatory structures are relatively short-lived, rapidly giving way to mechanisms designed to impose severe constraints on any independent initiatives. Tanzania took steps to begin a process of participatory development after the 1967 Arusha

Declaration. These included State control of the major means of production, administrative decentralisation and collectivisation into *ujamaa* villages. Yet it has been argued that, only five years later, these were replaced by rather more dictatorial procedures in which 'the participatory functions of the people's organisations were given peripheral attention' (Mushi 1981, p. 238)

The case of Ethiopia also illustrates well the ease with which participatory ideals are sacrificed to the goal of rapid political mobilisation and the push for economic development. The speed of the country's socialist revolution is reflected in the fact that, in the space of only three years, over 28,000 peasants' organisations with a total membership of 7.3 million households were formed (Abate and Teklu 1982). Peasant participation was, according to the revolutionary rhetoric, a fundamental part of the transformation process. Yet the peasant associations were controlled by urban-based government agents or *zemecha* who allowed the peasants only a 'nominal participation' in their running (Oakley and Marsen 1984, pp. 54–5). Furthermore, the peasantry had no say in determining post-revolutionary development strategies in rural areas.

The People's Republic of China is often cited as the best example of a nation which has successfully combined central planning with participatory development in the countryside. Yet even if there has been a relatively high degree of popular consensus regarding land reform and the collectivisation of agriculture, it is now recognised that local policy decisions at commune level were strongly influenced by party pressures, indicating a large degree of top-down manipulation. In fact, the lack of participation was one of the factors which led to the introduction in 1979, of the 'production responsibility system'. The authoritarian structures of the communes removed any freedom of action from the peasantry and 'the command economy was thrust right down to the village level, where peasant property and resources were allocated by the cadres as if they were the property of the State' (Gray 1984, p. 12). The impracticability of Mao's belief in the moral and economic necessity of collective agriculture has led to the changeover which now permits individual profit once obligations towards the State have been met. The responsibility system has turned out to be not only more productive but also more democratic, allowing greater discussion and popular participation at local level (Gray 1982, pp. 39–43). The question is, whether this reversion to the traditional Chinese concept of 'central supervision, local management' will be preserved through informal democratic mechanisms at local level and to what extent, and at what price, this less manipulative form of participation will speed up economic progress.

Co-operatives have become a popular tool of rural development and channel for people's participation. The establishment of official co-operatives proceeded rapidly during the 1950s and 60s and, based on the original Western model, were seen as a form of organisation which would allow members to exercise a degree of control over production and distribution of produce and inputs. Yet any illusions about popular involvement in co-operative decision-making were soon shattered. Far from being vehicles for democratic participation, co-operatives have generally been used to promote government policies and extend State control over the countryside. Rather than acting as agents of change for the benefit of the mass of poor farmers, co-operatives have become dominated by wealthier producers who are able to exercise their economic, political and social influence to monopolise internal management as well as government services such as subsidised credit and technical assistance (UNRISD 1975). Even in the famous Comilla community project, new co-operatives created specifically to aid poor farmers were soon 'dominated by the rich farmer moneylender–trader class', while the pressing problems of marginal and small cultivators were ignored (Haque *et al.* 1977, p. 93). Although such formal organisations have brought additional benefits to the poor, these have been unequally distributed and have not, on the whole, facilitated popular participation. They may even worsen the position of the poorest groups of producers (FAO 1979). The majority of such institutions could thus be classed as manipulative although, as indicated below, it may be possible to improve beneficiary participation in decision-making for the purpose of official development programmes provided that reforms of existing procedures are undertaken.

A more recently conceived and promising area of rural development strategy which permits greater peasant participation in State-directed programmes is that of farming systems research (FSR). Developed at a variety of centres over the past decade in Africa, Asia and Latin America, FSR was created as a response to the failure of traditional reductionist research methods to have any significant impact on improving small farmer agriculture. It starts from the proposition that small farmers' decisions are rational and seeks to increase productivity by developing technology and support systems which are fully acceptable to the recipients. It is thus a holistic approach which tries to understand 'the interdependencies and inter-relationships between the technical and human elements in the farming system' (Norman 1978, p. 5). This involves developing an understanding of the whole range of constraints – technical, economic, social and political – which influence peasant decision-making. An integral part of FSR is therefore a much closer, almost anthropological relationship between farmer and researcher/extensionist, entailing mutual respect and comprehension of the value of each other's knowledge, both modern and traditional (Clayton 1983; CIM-MYT economics staff 1984).

In so far as FSR allows for effective feedback of farmer opinion and to the extent that this influences subsequent policy-making, this approach can be labelled participatory. Yet there is an obvious danger that lip service will be paid to this more egalitarian system of learning, which is an essential prerequisite to developing a proper understanding of the problems facing poor cultivators. What Chambers (1983) calls 'reversals in learning' may be difficult to achieve within hierarchical planning structures dominated by narrow-minded technocrats and officials who have little concern for the constructive potential of traditional ideas and technology, and even less for dialogue with the poor.

Increasing State participation in rural development

The notion of State-guided participation, if somewhat self-contradictory, has played an increasingly important role within rural development strategies. As the examples quoted above have shown, it enables people and resources to be mobilised quickly and relatively cheaply for meeting nationally defined goals. The shortcomings of hastily thought out 'participatory' programmes are, however, legion. Not only do local communities suffer a loss of independence through the comprehensive adoption of top-down planning techniques, but internal village conflicts may be worsened and agricultural production may decline as a result of the disruption caused. Well-meant participatory ideals tend to be forgotten as the shortage of administrative manpower and trained technicians lead to the imposition of inappropriate measures which are poorly received by the rural populace, requiring further centralised direction and the threat of sanctions to guarantee implementation.

Yet in spite of these evident disadvantages, to completely reject the

idea of State-directed participation may be to throw out the baby with
the bathwater. Although the concept is undoubtedly manipulative to
varying degrees, depending on the case in question, there is certainly
room for increasing the level of people's involvement in rural development. Several broad options are open to planners. The first of these
concerns the adoption of a 'process' approach to management, in
contrast to the 'blueprint' style which has traditionally characterised
planning activities. Like farming systems research discussed above,
the process approach is based on the idea of a dialogue between
planners and beneficiaries in the search for appropriate measures. It
rejects the notion that projects are simply vehicles for the application
of preconceived solutions to development problems (Gow and
VanSant 1983, p. 432).

Unfortunately, most rural development schemes are characterised
by authoritarian, hierarchical management structures which allow
little or no beneficiary participation or information feedback. Large,
official irrigation projects tend to follow this pattern, as in the cases of
north-east Brazil (Hall 1978) and the Sudan (Barnett 1981). However,
there are exceptions, such as in the Philippines, where the National
Irrigation Administration has since 1976 developed a participatory
style and created strong irrigators' associations (Chambers 1983;
Bagadion and Korten 1985). The PIDER programme in Mexico is
another example which has encouraged farmer participation
throughout the project cycle (Cernea 1983), while similar principles
are also being extended to social forestry projects (Cernea 1981). As
Long clearly shows in Chapter Six of this volume, however, peasants
themselves adopt a variety of mechanisms and tactics to resist the
imposition of State controls, thus ensuring that they are not totally
'incorporated' or co-opted and that they maintain a degree of independence which is, paradoxically, *their* own way of 'participating' in the
development process.

Another option open to planners is that of decentralising certain
powers and functions in order to increase local control over policy-
making and resource application, including changes in the ways
bureaucracies operate in order to allow more local autonomy, what
have been called 'reversals in management' (Chambers 1983, p. 210).
Government must make resources available to local organisations
through revenue-sharing or block-grant arrangements in order that
they may take their own development initiatives. Yet the existence of powerful line ministries may preclude such an option, while

the monopolistic power of local elites may subvert participatory moves, especially if the government has little real control in the countryside.

Participation without the State

In a sense, these recommendations for increasing the level of beneficiary involvement in the planning and execution of official projects are doomed to failure almost from the start. Although there will always be welcome exceptions, the fact of the matter is that planning is still overwhelmingly characterised by the 'blueprint' approach described above, which allows no effective popular participation. It was argued that authentic participation is largely incompatible with State guidance. An alternative path is that which remains outside State tutelage, via non-government organisations (NGOs) and small-scale, participatory and locally-based schemes. In order to stress the contrast in methods and philosophy with official strategies, this unofficial approach has been labelled 'counterdevelopment' (Galjart 1981). Several major characteristics of this alternative have been highlighted, including the use of 'process learning' techniques based on dialogue mentioned above, the mobilisation of small groups as the basic units of action, the principle of self-reliance, local group control over project activities and the importance of collective action to solve group problems (Oakley and Marsden 1984). To this list could be added moves to prevent undue disparities of power and income within the target population (Galjart 1981).

The overriding feature of this concept of participation is that poor groups should be able to choose their own paths of action without State interference so that they represent an effective source of countervailing power which can challenge government authority when the people feel that this course of action is in their best interests. It means, in effect, to be able to exercise a degree of influence on the course of events within the process of planned rural development so that the traditionally underprivileged are not mere pawns but have an active influence over the allocation of resources. It is difficult to believe that governments would ever concede such autonomy to rural communities on a substantial scale. Conformity with national development priorities and the drive for political mobilisation are bound to perpetuate a far more manipulative and carefully controlled form of people's involvement.

There are plenty of examples of governments which have suppressed independent peasant initiatives when they clash with official goals. Coulson (1981) has described the case of the Ruvuma Development Association in Tanzania, one of the original models for the later *ujamaa* policy, yet which became so successful that it was banned as a threat to government authority. The farmers of Jamaane in Senegal took the initiative of forming a peasants' association and even hired an agronomist to advise them, but they clashed with the irrigation development authority which had other plans for their future (Adams 1981).

The only channel for pursuing the kind of 'empowering' participation under discussion here would therefore seem to be NGOs, many of which have a genuine commitment to changing the socio-political structures which underlie poverty and exploitation. It is customarily assumed that NGOs play an insignificant role in the total picture of rural development actions. While their contribution is undoubtedly much smaller than official organisations in terms of the total volume of expenditure, their influence is much greater than is generally imagined. In the first place, the role performed by unofficial bodies in educating and informing the wider public about development issues is of far greater importance than that of government institutions. In the area of foreign aid, for example, NGOs are frequently the first to highlight politically sensitive issues such as the structural roots of poverty and to fund controversial schemes which official aid bodies would be reluctant to support. Given their relative freedom from concern over diplomatic niceties and commercial profit, NGOs can finance the sorts of project which are more likely to challenge government policy. Secondly, and again in the area of foreign assistance, the sheer volume of NGO aid is far greater in relation to official aid than is generally realised. It has been calculated that the real ratio of government to non-government assistance is 6:1 rather than the 10:1 generally referred to (Lissner 1977). Clearly, only a proportion of this aid will be applied to projects which could be classed as participatory in the more radical sense, yet it does represent a significant and increasing trend in the overall pattern of aid disbursement for rural development.

There are literally hundreds of small-scale development schemes funded by NGOs which could be cited in support of this argument, ranging in size from the smallest of groups to regional programmes. Even official institutions, frustrated with the slow progress and uncertain benefits of conventional methods, are experimenting with the idea of smaller schemes. The People's Participation Programme, recently launched by the FAO, is an example of this. Some governments, including the British, channel a portion of their aid through NGOs under co-funding arrangements. However, given the political and diplomatic constraints under which official aid institutions operate, there must of necessity be severe restrictions on the extent to which they can become involved in supporting more radical projects characterised by a more authentic participation.

One of the best examples of a large-scale project of this nature is the Bhoomi Sena (Land Army) movement in Maharashtra State, India, which has united tribal and other poor groups in the region. It arose out of the nation-wide land seizure movement of the late 1960s in which the tribal leader Kaluram and his colleagues helped organise poor villagers to recuperate land usurped by the moneylenders– traders or *sawkars*. By the late 1970s the movement had become more widespread and systematic, enforcing the payment of legal minimum wages and investigating the situation of small cultivators. Through a process of dialogue and Freirian 'conscientisation' the movement has spread to over 120 villages, formed an agricultural workers' union and, in 1978, managed to get its candidate elected to the Maharashtra State Assembly (de Silva *et al*. 1982).

Many other cases exist of individual projects or movements which have, through a process of participatory development, enabled poor producers and their families to win benefits or concessions that would not otherwise have been forthcoming if they had been forced to rely on official benevolence. In north-east Brazil, for example, fisherwomen instituted a process of analysis through group meetings and a dialogue along Freirian lines with the help of an intermediary organisation, which produced marked changes in their attitudes and behaviour. This resulted in concrete moves by the fisherwomen to register themselves with the authorites, gain legal documentation and thus become entitled to stand for election on the local Board in order to represent their own interests for the first time (Oakley and Marsden 1984). Numerous other examples could be quoted from all over the world, from the Rangpur Self-Reliant Movement in Bangladesh (Haque *et al*. 1977) to the six cases analysed in India and Latin America by Oakley and Winder (1981) all of which preserve, to varying degrees, a certain independence from government control and freedom to determine their own courses of action.

The apparent advantages which unofficial interventions offer over government action for promoting participatory rural development should not, however, be allowed to obscure the fact that these initiatives have their own drawbacks. A major criticism is that projects sponsored and run by voluntary organisations tend to be small and geographically dispersed. Indeed, this feature is virtually a prerequisite for a successful participatory project, given the problems of bureaucratisation and access by the poor which become serious as organisations grow in size. Other criticisms relate to the general methods used to set up and run small development projects.

One of the major techniques employed in working with small groups is that of 'conscientisation', developed by Paulo Freire in north-east Brazil during the late 1950s and early 1960s (Freire 1972). It is an educational method which assumes, implicitly at least, that the poor have an imperfect knowledge of their own reality and that their social and political awareness must be heightened as a basis for group action in pursuit of developmental goals. While attractive to many individual and institutional practitioners of development, particularly in Latin America but also in India and Africa, this idea has been heavily criticised for assuming that 'lower-class people do not understand their own situation, that they are in need of enlightenment on the matter and that this service can be provided by selected higher-class individuals' (Berger 1977, pp. 137–8).

If outsiders can be criticised for underestimating the capacity of the poor for autonomous action, development workers can also be justly accused of frequently assuming a much greater potential degree of solidarity than is actually the case. Community 'animators' or 'facilitators' often adopt a manipulatory role, consciously or otherwise, and seek to impose their own politicised view of the world on to the poor, taking for granted a high degree of collective agreement over goals and ignoring internal conflicts. As with traditional community development, there is a very real danger that such patronising attitudes merely increase the dependency of the poor on external support, limit villagers' freedom of choice and make projects less participatory than would be desirable.

On balance, then, a systematic consideration of the concept of 'participation' has shown that it is a multi-faceted and at times highly nebulous concept which has often been misapplied to describe a range of development initiatives in the Third World. While most, if not all State-backed schemes are to a greater or lesser extent manipulatory,

NGO-funded programme perhaps offer more scope for genuinely participatory development, bearing in mind that this approach is also open to serious criticism from the point of view of maximising authentic involvement of beneficiaries. Whatever the strategy adopted, the most important consideration is to avoid falling into the trap of believing that increasing the level of people's participation is the key to successful development. Although it certainly is a major contributory factor which has recently been given much prominence in development literature, it should not be allowed to detract from a sustained attack on the structural obstacles which continue to hinder progress for the poor majority of the world's population.

Sociological perspectives on agrarian development and State intervention

This chapter provides a critical assessment of three contrasting analytical approaches to agrarian development, giving special attention to theoretical interpretations of the nature of State intervention. I have chosen to focus the discussion in this way in order to avoid getting trapped in the quicksands of the general debate on theories of the State. Linking issues like this offers a useful framework for elucidating certain key theoretical problems on the determinants of agrarian change and the role assigned farmers as against intervening parties in shaping the outcomes of intervention. A related issue is the need to develop ways of analysing how development policy is transformed during the implementation process. The last part of the chapter attempts to tie together these theoretical and practical policy questions by identifying the rudiments for developing a comparative analysis of development interface situations.

Contrasting analytical approaches to agrarian development and State intervention

Broadly speaking, one can distinguish between three different models: the logic of capital approach, the institutional incorporation model, and the actor-oriented view.

The logic of capital and commoditisation

This approach examines how the peasantry becomes progressively embedded in commodity markets through the sales of products and labour, and through the purchase of basic necessities and services. The process is said to be facilitated by government policy concerning rural taxation, the employment of labour for the building of infrastructure and the promotion of development projects aimed at increasing commercial production. The main result of this process is that peasant enterprise is gradually undermined and becomes intimately tied into the functioning of the logic of capitalist markets and institutions, although the degree of subsumption and autonomy of the household or farm enterprise will necessarily vary somewhat. The commoditisation model assumes that all forms of production become locked into the capitalist framework. There is no problem of the articulation of modes of production: all forms of labour process produce surplus value, either directly or indirectly. Thus the continued existence of non-wage forms of labour can be accommodated within this model: since it is assumed that generalised commodity exchange exists, non-capitalist labour processes are, by the same token, part of the same system. Agricultural development therefore entails increasing capital penetration, although it may not lead immediately to the formation of a capitalist farming class. Indeed, some writers have argued for the viability of simple commodity forms of production within a structure of dualism, entailing the coexistence and interrelations of both large and small-scale enterprise. Depending upon the particular circumstances, agricultural development is also frequently marked by the polarisation of rich and poor farmers implying the marginalisation of some producers, depeasantisation and proletarianisation (see Bernstein 1977, 1986 and Long *et al.* 1986 for a fuller exposition of these issues).

Models of this type are essentially concerned with the isolation of what one might call the 'central tendencies' of agrarian change. The approach aims to identify and characterise the general direction, paths, or stages of structural change, and to specify the factors responsible for this change. One of the best known examples of this approach for understanding agricultural development and policy is that by de Janvry (1981). He opens his analysis by pointing out that he believes the problems of agricultural production and poverty cannot simply be explained in terms of the characteristics of the agrarian sector (e.g. the problems of agricultural markets or terms of trade), or by reference to farmer behaviour or processes at the village or farm level (e.g. the limitations of land tenure systems or farm size). These issues, he argues, must instead be related to (a) the nature of the class structure of peripheral economies and (b) the process of capital accumulation which 'guides the historical development of capitalism' (de Janvry 1981, p. 8).

De Janvry's analysis centres upon analysing agrarian problems and processes in terms of how they form part of a world-wide structure composed of centre and peripheral economies that have unequal relations of dominance. Peripheral economies do not have their own *sui generis* reality and their own distinct laws of motion but form part of – or as de Janvry (1981, p. 22, my italics) put it, *'only a phase in'* – a pattern of capital accumulation on a world scale. They differ, however, from centre economies by being 'socially disarticulated' in that the different branches of production and consumption are not dynamically interrelated. What this means concretely is that semi-subsistence peasants participate in the modern economy through producing crops for marketing or through temporary wage labour, but do not participate significantly in the consumption of modern goods (which include not only consumer goods but also modern social and economic infrastructure). Hence there is little effective pressure resulting from changes in the consumption needs and demands of workers to increase wages or improve production conditions. This enables capital to minimise the costs of production. Related to this is what de Janvry calls 'functional dualism', whereby the peasant sector is functionally tied to the needs of the modern capitalist sector through the provision of both cheap food and labour. This, together with the weak development of the capital goods sector, enables the periphery to export cheap raw materials and wage goods, and the capitalist to maintain high rates of profit.

The major difficulty with de Janvry's formulation is that, while pinpointing certain crucial dimensions of Third World underdevelopment (e.g. the role of cheap labour, dualism and income inequalities between the peasant and export-linked sectors), it interprets the pattern of agrarian development in peripheral economies as resulting from the logic of capital accumulation, thus according little attention to other factors such as the styles of political intervention and ideologies of development represented by State programmes, or the influence of forms of peasant organisation or resistance. He also promises a class analysis but gives only a very schematic picture of the types of production enterprises and rural social classes (and the degrees of control they exercise over the State) in different agrarian situations. His main emphasis is on identifying the main paths to development in agriculture, namely the 'junker' (modernised estate) and the 'farmer' roads, and in arguing that changes in the social relations of production have been driven by the continous quest for cheap labour under disarticulated accumulation (1981, p. 94).

A further problem signalled here that is buried within de Janvry's elegant formulation is the spectre of a Leninist view of change whereby the peasantry exists but is gradually being destroyed, implying that functional dualism is a 'stage' in capitalist development. Throughout there is also an emphasis on the 'necessity' of certain structural changes and processes, and little attention given to analysing the actual struggles that emerge between different social classes and interests and the ways in which these shape agrarian structures. De Janvry's approach, then, suffers from the same fundamental theoretical inadequacies as much Marxist writing on development: it assumes, firstly, that 'the salient features of capitalist national economies and social formations can be derived or 'read off' from the concept of the capitalist mode of production and its laws', and secondly, it accords certain abstract entities, like capitalism or the concept of the 'disarticulated peripheral economy', 'with the capacity to shape socio-economic relations in accordance with their 'needs' ' (Booth 1985, pp. 776, 777).

The State as an instrument for resolving crises of capitalist accumulation
De Janvry attempts to avoid the pitfalls of adopting too mechanistic a view of the role of the State in agrarian development (see de Janvry 1981, pp. 183–7, where he attempts to reconcile 'instrumentalist' and 'structuralist' interpretations of the capitalist State; also de Janvry 1983, pp. 191–3; and de Janvry 1981, p. 233, where he stresses the value of considering 'individual and class agents' and their subjective visions of contradictions). Yet the overriding theoretical emphasis in his interpretation is the notion that policy shifts must ultimately be seen as responses to the needs and structural crises of capital accumulation in the global system. One basic feature of capitalism is its unplanned character with periodic crises. This causes a slowing down of accumulation leading to problems of unemployment and a fall in real wages. Since individual capitalists or even particular branches of capital are generally unable to offer much of a corrective to these processes, it falls to the State to devise measures in an attempt to restore profit levels and to ease social tensions. Although in the end the capacity of the State to resolve these problems is limited, the State is forever designing strategies for dealing with economic and legitimacy crises. De Janvry uses this approach to explain a series of

'reformist' measures developed in Latin America during the 1960s
and 1970s for dealing with the mounting 'agrarian crisis'. The crisis
was marked by strikingly uneven regional and sectoral development,
massive rural poverty, stagnation in food production, and increasing
political conflict. His argument is that each rural development initiative (which ranged from community development, the Green Revolution, land reform, integrated rural development and 'basic needs'
policies) represented a different mode of tackling some of these problems, and was directed towards somewhat different target groups.

Dominant class interests, represented either directly or indirectly
in State power, were critical in determining the types of policies
adopted and their effectiveness. Stated policy goals often concealed
other implicit (or what de Janvry calls 'real') objectives that were
'logically derived from the dominant characteristics and contradictions of the socio-economic system' (de Janvry 1981, pp. 232, 233).
Thus, depending upon the specific agrarian conditions, the capitalist
landed elite or the rural bourgeoisie (often in alliance with members of
the urban bourgeoisie) received the lion's share of the benefits.
Although at times some Latin American States moved to protect the
properties and social interests of sections of the peasantry (e.g. in an
attempt to limit the encroachment of large-scale capitalist agriculture), such measures ultimately helped to reproduce the pattern of
functional dualism which de Janvry considers central to the functioning of peripheral economies. Similarly, the State played a major
role in eliminating the 'remnants of precapitalist social relations,
which block[ed] the development of the forces of production.' For
example, the Peruvian land reform of 1969 modernised the export-
oriented estates leading to the consolidation of middle-size commercial farms on the coast and the formation of worker co-operatives;
whilst in the highlands the reform destroyed the semi-feudal estates
and accelerated the processes of socio-economic differentiation and
proletarianisation. The principal rhetoric of this reform was 'co-
operativism', 'peasant participation' and 'equity', but its implicit aims
(in hindsight largely unsuccessful) were to increase central control
over the rural population and to dynamise production (see Caballero
1980; de Janvry 1981, pp. 136–40; Long and Roberts 1984, pp.
248–55). De Janvry sees such 'missions of the capitalist State in the
periphery' as 'the principal purpose of the land reform programmes in
Latin America' (de Janvry 1981, p. 192).

De Janvry's account, then, accords relatively little autonomy in decision-making to State policy-makers and planners in shaping economic and social relationships within peripheral capitalist society. Indeed, he argues explicitly that the 'relative autonomy of the State is lessened in the periphery as the State becomes *a more direct instrument of domination of the class alliance in power*' (de Janvry 1981, pp. 192–3, my italics). Even the so-called 'bureaucratic-authoritarian' State (like that of Brazil or Argentina during certain periods – see O'Donnell 1978), which uses repressive means to contain the masses, remains, according to de Janvry, an instrument of class rule for a part of the bourgeoisie. There is hardly any discussion in his analysis of policy options, the nature of political and bureaucratic leadership, or of the well-documented phenomenon of the expansion of bureaucratic institutions and control in Latin America. De Janvry and many other writers within this school of thought tend to treat the notion of the State in a rather abstract, reified manner, sometimes suggesting the image of a unitary structure geared to the needs of capitalist expansion. Thus the State is said to respond directly to the dominant class, or to the interests of an alliance with foreign classes. It is only at times of crises in capital accumulation that the State is seen to be somewhat independent from the direct influence of dominant classes, although as de Janvry would argue this may be more apparent than real. Hence the capitalist State in centre and peripheral economies is fundamentally driven and structured by what Poulantzas (1973) calls 'the objective power of capital'.

In this schema, the whole question of the 'relative autonomy' of the State apparatus (i.e. the administrative elite and State agencies) *vis-à-vis* the dominant classes is left unresolved. The main reason for this is that the explanation of State activities and policies does not go beyond the general idea of how these can be seen to contribute to the process of capital accumulation and to crisis management. There is no attempt to identify the limits of dependence by particular types of State on the bourgeoisie or other classes and to examine the conditions under which particular State agencies are able to operate autonomously. The latter would necessitate a detailed study of how different agencies are subject to various political influences which, of course, leads to a much more differentiated view of State structures. It also requires an understanding of the social composition of the bureaucracy and the organisational means and sets of interests, both bureaucratic and private, that shape the formulation and outcomes of policy. A further important field of enquiry concerns the differential local responses to development programmes, since the results of a single or similar policy often turn out quite different in different countries or regions of a country. Indeed, one of the most disturbing aspects of de Janvry's interpretation of 'reformist' policies is that he demonstrates the similarities in their structural role, but fails to elucidate the important differences in their means of implementation and context-specific outcomes.

The institutional incorporation model

A second perspective on agrarian change is that which centres upon the concept of 'incorporation'. According to Pearse (1975), incorporation implies the integration of rural populations into the wider national framework through the impact of urban centres, the extension of communications and government bureaucracy, and through the commercialisation of production. This urban-propelled expansion entails new institutional developments aimed at modernising production and establishing more effective forms of economic organisation and administrative control.

Institutional development forms the core of Benvenuti's (1975) analysis of how farm enterprises become integrated into the wider technological and administrative environment. Benvenuti argues that the immediate task-oriented environment of the farmer, made up of institutions and officials representing government and farmers' organisations, comes to have a determining influence on farmer behaviour and on farm enterprise decisions. These various external institutions, which may include banks, the agricultural extension service, farm suppliers, credit and marketing organisations, co-operatives and farmers' organisations, provide the norms for and prescribe the conduct of farmers in the realm of economic decision-making and in relation to technical and organisational solutions to farming problems. They become indispensable conditions for the functioning of the farming enterprise (by providing capital, advice and markets) and they constrain the choices and independence of the farmer. Benvenuti goes as far as to suggest that eventually farmers experience a new kind of 'feudal vassalage' whereby they merely follow the instructions of the technical experts and bend to the wishes of credit agencies and other input-providers.

Benvenuti's account of the incorporation of farms into this institutional system challenges the traditional idea that farmers are autonomous decision-makers who operate in a free market governed by an invisible hand. His view is that decision-making in fact shifts to external institutions, thus undermining the independent management functions of the farmer and integrating the farm into a wider operational unit or 'system of production'. This wider operational system is based upon a network of formal economic institutions, such as banks and private firms, as well as government service agencies, and possibly also farmers' co-operatives or State collectives (Benvenuti and Mommaas 1985). These various external institutions knit together to form a network in which the measures and regulations confronted by the farmer are co-ordinated. The farmer himself gradually perceives this system of links as some kind of quasi-organisation with central decision-making located at the top and implementation at the bottom.

Although the degree to which the farmer or farms is incorporated will vary, the central tendency, then, is towards externalisation of farm practice: an increasing number of farm tasks are separated from the farm labour process and reallocated to external agencies. Thus tasks that were initially organised and co-ordinated under the direct command of the farmer himself (e.g. seed selection, animal feed production, the organising of necessary inputs such as fertilisers and water application, and the marketing of products) are now co-ordinated through the newly-established system of technical and administrative relations, and through commodity exchange. This increasing externalisation, as van der Ploeg (1986) has shown, not only affects production activities but also results in the complete reshaping of the process of reproduction. The expansion or simple reproduction of the farm becomes more and more market-dependent; and in this regard the pattern of institutional externalisation described by Benvenuti concurs with Bernstein's commoditisation model.

Benvenuti further argues that the modernisation of agriculture tends towards increasing 'scientification', as shown by developments in technology in the form of hybrid seed and new chemical inputs. Externalisation, scientification and increasing vertical integration of farm production constitute, then, the three principal elements of the process of technical and administrative incorporation. Although the degree of incorporation will vary, depending on the context, modern farming in the Third World, as elsewhere, increasingly takes this form. One notes, for example, the increasing role played by special agencies set up by the State to promote integrated rural development programmes and to establish quality-controlled production for export. Transnationals and agribusinesses assume an important role in the organisation and processing of such agricultural production, to the extent that Sanderson (1986, p. 25) emphasises that, for instance, in Mexico we now have a pattern of thoroughly 'international agriculture'. This new pattern marginalises the farmer even more since private companies or State enterprise may operate contract farming and rental systems in order to have firmer control over the planning and carrying out of production tasks. Frequently, co-operatives and farmers' organisations perform similar functions.

In contrast to the logic of capital approach to agrarian development, Benvenuti provides a general format for describing the process of intervention itself. He emphasises that intervention in agriculture consists of a set of institutions that impinge upon the farm unit. This institutional complex acquires its own co-ordinated rationality in that the various institutions develop a high degree of consensus concerning the diagnosis and solution of problems faced by the farmer, and in terms of a commitment towards promoting technological development and commercial production. The process is accompanied by increased centralisation by the State and is therefore common to both capitalist and socialist economies.

The State as an administrative and coordinating authority   Underlying Benvenuti's account of institutional incorporation is a Weberian picture of the State. According to this view, the State is defined as an enduring executive and administrative apparatus that makes authoritative decisions and exercises control over a given territory and people. Hence 'the State properly conceived is no mere arena in which socio-economic [or class] struggles are fought out, but it is rather a set of administrative, policing and military organisations headed or more or less coordinated by an executive authority . . .' These organisations 'are the basis of State power as such' (Skocpol 1979, p. 29). Benvenuti arrives at the same conclusion in relation to intervention processes in agriculture.

This perspective on the State contrasts with Marxist theory since it does not view the State as merely an analytical aspect of abstractedly conceived modes of production, nor is it defined as an alliance of political control that reflects and reproduces the dominant class or particular class interests and relations. State policy therefore is not derivative simply of class relationships. Indeed, under certain conditions, the State, including in this both the State apparatus consisting of the civil and military bureaucracy, on the one hand, and those having formal control of this apparatus, the government, on the other, may exhibit relative autonomy from dominant national and international class interests.

Another feature of Benvenuti's interpretation is that it suggests a 'corporatist' view of intervention in agriculture which assumes a considerable degree of integration among the institutions of the farmers' environment, even to the extent of suggesting that farmers' organisations and co-operatives representing local producer groups acquire the same rationality and objectives as State or private institutions. Hence the institutional system encompassing the farmer becomes part of 'the extended State' which integrates socio-economic producer groups into the governmental system through a system of organised representation; just in the same way as labour unions and employers' associations become 'governing institutions' (Winkler 1976). Benvenuti's line of argument therefore seems to attribute considerable co-ordinating power to the State bureaucracy: only the State, it seems, is in a position to determine the rules of the game and establish the working relations between the parties concerned.

Although Benvenuti's scheme is interesting for the emphasis it places upon the organisational dimension, it fails in fact to examine the nature of bureaucratic organisation and relationships and makes the unwarranted assumption that the institutions and development agencies involved in constructing the farmer's institutional and technological environment fit together coherently and present a concerted attack on the autonomy of the farm enterprise. There is no appreciation of the importance of inter-agency conflict or of the struggles that take place between farmers' organisations and government or private institutions. A related problem is the failure to locate the discussion within an analysis of existing power structures at either regional or national level.

A passive peasantry and bureaucracy?　The two foregoing models of agrarian development present alternative ways of conceptualising the increasing encapsulation of farming populations: the first focusing upon the expansion of commodity markets and capital penetration, and the second on the impact of various rural institutions set up to serve the farmer by organising production inputs and outputs. Although both approaches mention the important role played by State agencies and other organisations, neither approach attempts to analyse the types of interactions and negotiations that occur between the representatives of the various organisations and the farmers themselves. When they do refer to encounters between the State and local groups, no room is allowed for the ways in which farmers or peasants themselves attempt to structure the interfaces they are drawn into. Thus the image one receives is that of a passive peasantry faced by overwhelming external forces.

It is equally the case that these models show no interest in or sensitivity towards the ways in which the representatives of encapsulating institutions interpret their mandates and define their work tasks *vis-à-vis* the farming population. Benvenuti tends to assume that a common rationality and normative definition develops among implementors and organisational representatives, be they technicians or administrators. Bernstein writes rather simply about State policy and actions and the ways in which they facilitate capitalist expansion; and de Janvry follows a more structuralist line, arguing that the State (and therefore those that represent it) will generally act in the interests of capital accumulation, even if it means opposing the short-term interests of a dominant class or class alliance. Hence the bureaucrat or policy-maker is allocated an equally passive role.

All three writers would of course claim that they are making simplifying assumptions in order to develop coherent models. Nevertheless, it is my contention that in order to explain the differences that may arise, both within a defined farming population and between contrasting agrarian situations, it is necessary to look more closely at the sets of relationships that evolve between intervening agencies and local groups, and to make this a point of theorisation. Only then will we be able to establish more precisely the degrees of capital subsumption or institutional control exercised by the State or other external institutions *vis-à-vis* different categories of farmer. It will also help to give flesh and blood to the somewhat disembodied structures of the logic of capital and institutional incorporation.

An actor-oriented approach

An actor-oriented analysis of agrarian change goes some way to meeting these criticisms. Such an approach is based upon the idea of differential responses to changing circumstances. It assumes that there exist variations within agricultural systems such that we can expect different patterns of response and change. These different forms are in part created by the farmers themselves: farmers are not simply to be seen as passive recipients, but as actively strategising and interacting with outside institutions and personnel. The understanding of agrarian change is therefore complex and requires working from the very beginning with the concept of heterogeneity. Farmers and other local actors shape the outcomes of change. Change is not simply imposed upon them.

There are several versions of actor-oriented models: for example, decision-making, network, or exchange models (see Long 1977, pp. 105–43, for an overview of these). The common assumption underlying all of them is that different social patterns may develop within the same structural circumstances. For instance, van der Ploeg and Bolhuis (1985) have drawn the contrast between 'intensification' versus 'extensificiation' strategies that coexist within the same farming population in both Peru and Italy. These differences show how farmers cope differently with processes of commoditisation and institutional incorporation. Another example is my own study (Long 1968) of a group of small-scale commercial farmers in Zambia that exhibit differences in the mobilisation and organisation of labour which, I suggest, affects the long-term trajectory and viability of their farm enterprises. These differences among them were traced to a division within the community between Jehovah's Witness and non-Witness farmers. The former, building upon a network of social ties based upon church membership and restructured kinship relations, were able to develop more stable strategies for organising farm inputs. They also adhered to a stricter and more ascetic social code.

A third example is that of Bennett (1981) who analyses differences in farm management styles found among Canadian farmers. Bennett depicts the folk categories which farmers themselves use to describe differences in farm enterprise development and from this he shows that the 'best' manager from the point of view of local culture is not the farmer who follows economically ideal, maximising, management styles but the one who adapts these standards to his own operations. The latter are influenced by the stage of development of the farm enterprise, by his family needs, and by the constraints of the larger system.

Bennett shows that the management criteria used by the farmers are multiple, including farmer qualities, such as perseverance, sincerity, ability to juggle conflicting objectives, or possessing particular kinds of knowledge and skill, as well as estimates of production, income, and the conditions of the farm machinery, fields, fences, or stock. He is then able to show that some of these differences in styles and strategies are reflected quantitatively in different outcomes of production and farm development. He concludes that 'the extent that producers respond to the "right" signals [i.e. in accord with the economists market incentive models], in order to provide desired production magnitudes, is a rough measure of the extent to which they have assimilated the very frames of reference used by the economic analysts of the agricultural market. However, this response is never perfect, and often it varies widely (Bennett 1981, p. 234). In fact farm strategies are affected by many factors besides simple market incentives. Strategies vary according to stage of farm enterprise development and in rhythm with the family life-cycle. For example, although the area is considered highly suitable for specialised wheat production, farmers attempting to establish their farms frequently mix different types of production on a small scale in order to realise the benefits of diversification, whilst others in the same position opt for the more risky strategy of land acquisition and speculation. According to local folk terminology, the former are designated 'scramblers' and the latter 'land grabbers'. Similarly, bursts of investment in farm machinery and infrastructural improvement seem to be a feature of the point at which the transfer of the farm to the new generation is imminent.

Bennett's study, then, indicates the need to look more closely than either commoditisation or institutional models do at the ways in which farmers manage, not only their on-farm resources, but the sets of external relationships and institutions impinging upon them. These examples of studies of varying patterns of farm development could be further illustrated by reference to 'centralised' versus 'co-ordinated' patterns of organisation (Long and Richardson 1978, pp. 191–200), 'multiple enterprise' combining agricultural and non-agricultural activities (Long 1979), and long-term versus short-term production strategies (Ortiz 1973).

All this work stresses that, even if it is possible to isolate within a given agrarian structure or farming population a central tendency, it is important also to examine the minority patterns. The latter will have their own determinants or conjunctures of factors that are specific to scale, social composition of the farm or household, and to the objectives and values of the farmers in question. It is important therefore to explain the full distribution curve, not just the mean or medium. It is difficult to say which organisational form or strategy will actually be the most adapted to circumstances and to change over the long run. An adequate analytical approach to the study of agrarian change requires that we theorise the question of structural variance and differential responses to change. Change should not be assumed to be lineal or convergent; it may be backwards and forwards, divergent, cyclical, or zig-zagging, depending upon the historical circumstances.

An actor perspective also emphasises the importance of taking full account of 'human agency', which means recognising that individuals, whether they be farmers, peasants, landlords, bureaucrats or politicians, attempt to come to grips with the world around them, and that they do this both cognitively on the basis of existing categories, knowledge and forms of consciousness, and organisationally in the way they interact with other individuals and social groups. Farmers and other social actors are, within limits (i.e. given the information and uncertainties that exist), 'knowledgeable' and 'capable' (Giddens 1979, pp. 49–95). They devise ways of solving problematic situations they face, but are constrained by scarcity of resources, social commitments, differential power relations and cultural values and standards.

A further important feature of actor-oriented models is that, contrary to what is often supposed, they do not stop (either methodologically or theoretically) at the individual decision-making level. They require that we take account of the ways in which interacting individuals and social groups have a mutual influence upon each other. This leads to the consideration of what we may call 'intermediate' level structures, such as social networks, household confederations, farmers' organisations, systems of production tying the farmer into his institutional environment, and organised 'interface' structures that constitute the regular modes of interaction between farmers and public authorities.

An actor perspective on State policy and intervention   Applying this approach to questions of State intervention entails an entirely different way of formulating the problem from that of the two previous theoretical perspectives. All forms of external intervention necessarily enter the life-worlds of the individuals and groups affected and thus, as it were, comes to form part of the resources and constraints of the social strategies they develop. In this way so-called external factors are internalised and may come to mean quite different things to different interest groups or actors. Externally-originating factors

are therefore mediated, incorporated, and often substantially transformed by local organisational and cognitive structures. They are also
shaped by the ongoing exchanges and negotiations that take place
between farmers, other local actors, and the intervening agents. Close
attention must therefore be given to understanding how particular
interventions (e.g. a new agricultural technology or a land reform
programme) become modified or even completely transformed
through the interplay of local and extra-local structures and processes.

This process by which policy objectives are renegotiated at local or
regional level is well illustrated by the case, described by Winder
(1979), of a large-scale government-sponsored irrigation project in the
north-west of Mexico. The Mexican government had originally
planned to establish a collective *ejido* system for cultivation but,
under pressure from farmers, allowed them to subdivide into sectors
and small working groups. Government officials also turned a blind
eye to internal arrangements for distribution of profits on the basis of
plot yields instead of labour input, which had been the original
intention. They likewise abandoned having professional managers
heading each production co-operative when this was opposed, and
instead permitted the establishment of a system of locally-elected
peasant representatives. Yet despite these major modifications, when
central government or party officials visited the scheme, the farmers
would turn out in numbers to demonstrate the wonders of collective
production! Glavanis (1984, pp. 400–1) describes a similar set of
manoeuvres adopted by Egyptian peasants to avoid the compulsory
cultivation of cotton every three years.

Extending this type of analysis, Martinez (1983) shows how Mexican rural development programmes work out quite differently in
different regional settings. He argues that the presence of the State, in
the form of government agencies and numbers of government personnel (such as extension officers and other *técnicos*), varies according to
the type of regional economy and power structure. Some regional
elites, it appears, have greater leverage than others at national level;
and some of the more powerful agrarian regions have pursued
objectives that run counter to those of the federal government.
Indeed, as one provincial level planner recently commented to me,
'there is in fact no agrarian development policy, if by that we mean a
set of measures that are simply applied. Everything is negotiated
among the parties involved.'

Grindle's (1985) recent book on agrarian development represents an interesting attempt to tackle questions of State intervention from a fairly explicit actor perspective. However she concerns herself primarily with State elites and bureaucrats rather than with local producers or peasant groups. One theme she is interested in is the role and variable autonomy of State elites in the formulation and implementation of public policy. She shows that the executive and bureaucratic apparatus may pursue national development in opposition to the interests of any particular powerful group or class coalition or alliance. She argues that giving more emphasis to the 'public managers' enables one to focus on the development belief systems and development ideologies of policy-makers and planners, on the formulation and implementation of specific decisions, on the skills and influence of particular political leaders.

This leads to an analysis of the extent to which technocrats and public managers form an 'independent State' and allocate resources in a way that expands their own power and wealth. Emphasising these dimensions, she claims, helps one to account for the enormous expansion of the State apparatus itself. She does not assume the State to be either autonomous or monolithic. Rather, she is interested in the question of relative degrees of autonomy over time and across policy sectors and ministries. This does not ignore the fact that State elites are constrained by wider political and economic realities. State development policies may at any given time coincide with the interests of dominant groups but it is difficult to infer the domination of the State simply from the content or impact of the policy itself. Thus she argues against de Janvry by suggesting that policies to promote agrarian capitalism or land reform, for example, do not consistently result from the clear domination of the State by specific class interests (national or foreign). They have been influenced by the development ideologies adopted by the State elites, by the leadership of particular individuals, and by the political accommodations and bargains struck between State elites and other groups (especially in the private sector).

In her earlier study of CONASUPO, the Mexican government staple food marketing and service agency, Grindle (1977) uses an exchange model to analyse the ways in which bureaucrats develop strategies for pursuing both public and personal goals. She shows that informal exchanges tend to evolve into longer-term commitments between individuals of different hierarchical levels and to pyramid into networks of exchange alliance, resembling the patron-client pattern often described by anthropologists and political scientists for

Latin America (see, for example, the account of the Brazilian political patronage system by Leeds (1964); for a more sophisticated treatment of Mexican political networks and processes, see Carlos and Anderson 1981; de la Pena 1986). She documents the patterns of career mobility and the problems that arise because of the insecurity of job tenure produced by the Mexican *sexenio* (six-year presidential) system. She looks at the methods used for obtaining employment and the ways in which office chiefs, departmental heads, and others set about recruiting local subordinates, and using their public positions to enhance the power of the agency and its top administrators. She then examines how personal political alliances affect or are mobilised to bring about policy change.

Another aspect concerns policy implementation, primarily at provincial (Mexican state) level. In line with Martinez, she shows how central government policy is diluted or redefined at the state level as a result of the pressure from powerful local groups and because of the exigencies of responding to immediate situations of conflict and competition. Those states where CONASUPO offices were staffed by individuals directly dependent upon central office leadership for continued career mobility opportunities were those in which the most effective implementation of central policy took place.

Finally she looks at the delivery of the rural development programme at local level. Public officials working at grass roots level became intermediaries between the low income clients of the agency and the institution itself, in order to achieve a more rapid and adequate delivery of services. Again personal alliance structures were critical for the effectiveness of these brokers at local level. In the same way that 'successful' field officers formed part of the personal followings of their superiors, so did their peasant clients serve them. Grindle elucidates the dilemmas of the field officer but gives much less attention to analysing the peasant responses and strategies. Indeed the bottom end of the process is largely assumed rather than fully described and analysed. There is, for example, no adequate analysis of power relations and organisational resources and social expectations at the level of the peasantry. In fact the study virtually stops at the point of direct interface with the farmers.

A more recent study (Arce 1986; Arce and Long 1986) of the interaction between government field officers (*técnicos*) and peasants in an area of rural Mexico fills a number of gaps. It shows, for instance, how *técnicos* are often caught between two systems of knowledge (that of the administrator/technician and that of peasant villager) and that it becomes impossible for them to bridge these worlds, not least because the administrative unit to which the *técnicos* belong develops its own accommodations (through the influence of the boss and his network of support) to the situation. Arce's study provides a fuller picture of the way lower level, frontline government officials operate, their world view and development perspectives, their networks of influence, and the mechanisms for retaining control which include sending troublemakers (*grillosos*) to remote areas called 'punishment zones' (*areas de castigos*) when they do not conform to the working rules set by the administrative boss.

A modified pluralist view of the State   Grindle has a distinctive view of the nature of State authority. She firstly argues against simple notions of an alliance of domestic and foreign capital dominating the State and prescribing the nature and direction of State policy. She points out that reformist policies occasionally impinge upon dominant class interests, sometimes even curbing the operations of foreign capital, and at other times they might incorporate non-elite groups. A second important point is that State policies are not all that consistent and often not easily identifiable. While a given policy may benefit a specific group, others may infringe directly on the same group's interests. There are also unintended consequences of policy and many policies are adopted but never in fact implemented. Hence linking policy content and formally charged policy-making by a State elite to control exercised by domestic or international capitalist class interests poses difficult conceptual issues. In many respects State policy is an outcome of competing and conflicting interests among bureaucratic entities of the State itself, although Grindle is quick to acknowledge that this process is also influenced by the impact of wider economic and political forces.

In this respect her work combined a 'pluralist' approach (see Dahl 1961) that emphasises how government agencies and officials act as one set of pressure groups among many others, with an interest in examining the interaction between the bureaucratic elite and other elite groups in terms of their influence over State resources and policy. Such an approach has the advantage of focusing attention upon the ongoing processes of political bargaining that shape the formulation and implementation of policy. But in order to understand this process, it becomes important to situate this within the framework of a

structural analysis which takes full account of the structural constraints and pressures on policy-making.

Combining actor-oriented and structural modes of analysis   This pin-
points the central weakness of actor-oriented approaches to the study
of policy and State intervention, whether conducted at the level of
policy-makers and bureaucrats or at the level of State-peasant relations. Focusing upon actor strategies and transactions tends to deflect
interest from the structural context and from examining the
imperatives for change generated by the dynamic of the larger poli-
tico-economic structures. An actor-oriented analysis needs to be
combined with an understanding of wider structural phenomena,
since many of the choices perceived and strategies pursued by individuals and groups have been shaped by processes outside the immediate
arena of interaction (Harriss 1982, pp. 21–6). One useful approach to
understanding the effects of structural processes is that of political
economy, which focuses upon showing how economic processes and
the patterns of social organisation are structured by the larger framework of economic and political power relations, including the ways in
which the State attempts to control and manage the outcomes of
local-level development (see Bates 1983, pp. 134–47). Such an
approach also gives attention to analysing the social and ideological
mechanisms by which particular economic systems and types of 'production regime' (Burawoy 1985, pp. 7–8) are reproduced. Providing
one avoids the shortcomings of certain types of political economy (e.g.
de Janvry's tendency to accord primacy to the capitalist mode of
production and its 'laws' of development), then such an approach can
offer a useful conceptual framework for examining how structural
factors (such as changing market and international conditions, shifts
in the power exercised by particular classes at national or regional
level, or in international development ideology) affect State policy and
State-peasant relations.

Thus, an actor-oriented perspective, which emphasises the detailed
analysis of the struggles, negotiations, and exchanges occurring
within and between specific social groups, classes and networks of
individuals, is not, as some writers appear to suggest (e.g. Alavi 1973;
Harriss 1982, p. 27), antithetical to a structural analysis since it is
important also to take full account of the structural constraints on
choice and strategy (Long 1977, 1984). It becomes possible therefore
to integrate these two approaches into a single framework of analysis,

as we have attempted in our recent book on regional development in central Peru (Long and Roberts 1984).

The importance of developing an interface analysis of development encounters

One advantage in combining an actor perspective with a political economy analysis is that it facilitates an explanation of the differential responses to structurally similar circumstances. This aspect is crucial for exploring the allocative dimension of development policy. Planned interventions by public agencies aim to distribute the benefits in the form of resources, goods and services, or alternatively they selectively penalise, regulate, give permission, or withdraw resources. Thus they have distributive or redistributive effects. But in order to understand this allocative process it is necessary to go beyond the interests of those involved in influencing and formulating policy. Rather, one must look closely at how policy is implemented and at how the relevant actors (both implementors and target and non-target groups) interpret and react to it.

Differential responses are often influenced by existing ecological, demographic, organisational and cultural variations, but a further important aspect to consider is the process of intervention itself. Public agencies may formulate plans and well-prepared strategies of intervention but finally it falls to frontline workers to implement them. As many studies have shown (Batley 1983; Grindle 1980; Lipsky 1980; Warwick 1982), implementors always have discretion in the interpretation and performance of their tasks. This allows room for manoeuvre for them and their clients. Documenting the transactions and negotiations between specific local actors and implementors shows how particular individuals or households in fact face somewhat different intervention situations with different pay-offs. Planned intervention is an ongoing, socially constructed and negotiated process, not simply the execution of an already specified plan of action with predictable outcomes. The act of implementation itself frequently transforms policy.

In exploring these dimensions it is useful to identify the important social 'interfaces' linking local groups with the larger structure. I define 'social interfaces' as the critical points of intersection or linkage between different social systems or levels of social order, where structural discontinuities, based upon differences of normative values and social interest, are most likely to be found. The concept also implies some kind of face-to-face encounter between individuals or social units representing different interests and backed by different resources. The interacting parties are often differentiated in terms of power. There are several key aspects of interface analysis (see Brown 1983, for an analysis of organisational interfaces, especially pp. 19–46; Long 1984, for its relevance for policy analysis; Arce and Long 1986, for discussion of interfaces between knowledge systems):

1. It focuses upon the linkages that develop between the interacting individuals or parties rather than on the individuals themselves. Continued interaction encourages the development of boundaries and shared expectations that regulate the interaction of the participants such that the interface itself becomes an organised entity. For example, the interface between management and union representatives or between landlord and tenant persists in an organised way over time with rules, expectations and sanctions. The same is true of interfaces involving State officials and local peasant or farmer leaders, or those occurring between less formally constituted groups or social categories committed to somewhat different or opposing values or interests (e.g. interfaces based on differences of ethnicity, gender or age).

2. It draws attention to the forces making for conflict or incompatibility between the parties concerned. Although interface interactions presuppose some degree of common interest, they are also likely to generate conflict arising from contradictory interests and objectives. Negotiations at the interface are sometimes carried out by individuals who represent particular constituencies, groups or organisations. The roles of such representatives inevitably create ambiguities since the individuals concerned must respond to the demands of their own group, as well as to the expectations of those with whom they must negotiate.

3. It highlights differences in world views or cultural interpretations between the interacting parties or individuals. For example, the cultural assumptions and views on development expressed by agricultural extension workers and farmers often do not coincide; and the same holds for individuals working in different capacities within a government bureaucracy. Such differences are not merely idiosyncratic but reflect differences in patterns of socialisation and professionalisation. The result is often miscommunication or a clash of rationalities

(Chambers 1983; Box 1984). The process is further complicated by the coexistence of several different cultural models (associated with persons of differing age, sex or status) within a given population or administrative organisation.

4. It demonstrates the need to look at processes of intervention diachronically. Interfaces change their character over time due to, among other things, shifting internal and external relationships and to changing perceptions, resources and commitments. This diachronic process is partly short-term in that any changes that take place immediately affect the actors concerned, but also longer-term in that interface encounters develop their own ground rules and styles of interaction and organisation which can generate cumulative effects, leading to a restructuring of the interface itself or to the creation of new ones. In order to understand these processes, the detailed analysis of social interaction must be situated within a broader appreciation of institutional frameworks and power fields (for more extended discussion see Long 1984, pp. 10–13).

5. Interface analysis should not therefore focus exclusively on the detailed study of the patterns of social interaction that take place between the specific actors involved. It should provide the means of identifying those groups, individuals or social categories excluded from particular interfaces, thus highlighting the existence of systematic forms of non-interaction characteristic of marginalised groups such as the poorer peasants or categories of women.

6. On yet another level, interface analysis can contribute to the general discussion of State–peasant relations in the Third World (see, for example, Hyden 1980; Bernstein 1981; Spittler 1983; Geschiere 1984). Interface studies reveal concretely the nature of State–peasant relations in particular localities or regions. They also help to identify how much political space there exists for local initiatives aimed at changing the pattern of resource distribution or at improving the benefits received by local groups, and in this way they facilitate an understanding of the character and significance of specific types of State structure and policy. In contrast, as Skocpol (1979, pp 31–2) has pointed out, general theories of the State often operate at a high level of abstraction and tend towards the reification of State institutions and action.

Conclusions: contrasting views of State intervention

The foregoing discussion has covered a broad field of theoretical and methodological issues relating to the study of agrarian development viewed from three contrasting perspectives. One central concern has been to identify the different visions of State intervention and policy projected by these different approaches. The first approach – the logic of capital model – interprets the actions of the capitalist State in terms of the imperatives and 'logic' of capitalist development, stressing how State power-holders and institutions function to secure the long-term survival of capitalist forms of accumulation, thus safeguarding the interests of the dominant class or class alliance. This process is complicated by the fact that capital accumulation on a global scale is subject to periodical crises that require corrective measures by the State. Hence the State may institute policies that have negative consequences for certain segments of the dominant class or class alliance, and that offer concessions to subordinate groups such as peasant producers or workers. It is at these historical junctures that the State is said to acquire some measure of independent action or 'relative autonomy' *vis-à-vis* the influence of the dominant class, although in the end the 'objective power of capital' and the shoring up of the system works to the benefit of capitalist interests, national and foreign.

One unresolved issue in this line of reasoning is the question of State autonomy (see Hamilton 1982, pp. 8–13). Since analysis is essentially directed towards revealing the underlying structure and laws of motion of capitalism, it becomes difficult on general theoretical grounds to allow much room for independent action by the State, if by this we mean action against the interests of the dominant class which can ultimately result in fundamental changes in the existing capitalist mode of production. In order to resolve this, one needs to define more precisely the sets of social forces impinging upon State power-holders and institutions and to determine the means and extent of control exercised by powerful interest groups, including the dominant national and foreign classes (see Miliband 1969 for a discussion of the mechanisms used by the dominant class: for example, obtaining positions in State institutions, membership of key committees, lobbying, campaigning, and controlling the media). The question of State autonomy and the interpretation of State policies and outcomes, therefore, requires grounding historically and contextually in order to specify the nature and significance of the organisations, interests, resources, and class actors represented.

Structuralist explanations of the de Janvry kind fall short of this in a number of ways. They explain the general conditions and vicissitudes of capitalist development in the periphery, indicating how these set limits for the actions of the State, but fail to consider the interests and strategies of the State managers involved in the formulation and/or implementation of policy. They introduce the notion of 'real' or 'implicit' policy objectives, a concept which is impossible to pin down except by reference to some assumed hidden logic. However, they do not attempt to deal with the significance of the unanticipated consequences of State intervention, nor with the differential responses at local or regional level, dimensions that are critical for interpreting outcomes and the implementing capacities of particular State formations. One draws the conclusion, then, that the logic of capital approach to State intervention does not differentiate sufficiently between what one might call the 'imperatives' and the 'actualities' of capitalist development as they work out in differing social (agrarian) contexts. There is also the tendency to reify State institutions and actions and, consequently, to neglect the importance of such processes as inter-agency, inter-ministry, or inter-group struggles in the determination and execution of policy.

The second analytical approach focuses upon the process of institutional incorporation whereby farmers or local groups become integrated into the wider technico-administrative environment consisting of various State and non-State organisations. Incorporation is depicted in terms of three interconnected processes: 'externalisation' which describes how production tasks are increasingly taken over by external bodies, 'scientification' which identifies the growing importance of modern technology, and increased 'centralisation' by the State. The latter process functions to co-ordinate the interrelations between the various institutions and assists in resolving conflicts that might arise between the different interest groups (e.g. peasant farmers, extensionists, bankers and farmers' associations). The institutional incorporation model is essentially Weberian in its stress on the significance of modern forms of organisation, technology and rationality. However, unlike Weber, it is more concerned with the nature of the institutional environment surrounding the producer than with the characteristics of bureaucratic institutions *per se*. It aims to show how integration into an external network of institutions, which develop their own coordinated rationality, undermines independent forms of production and decision-making.

Although the concept of the State remains underdeveloped, the implication seems to be that modernisation entails increasing forms of corporatism, whereby the State makes a pact with various socio-economic interest groups to bring them into the process of planning, sometimes even allowing them space to determine their own affairs. This suggests that the State is essentially made up of a complex set of organisations, backed by executive power, which aims to control territory and people. Since many different social interests are represented which directly or indirectly shape the actions of the State, one cannot argue that State policies are simply derivative of either class relationships and struggles or the logic of capital accumulation.

A major difficulty with the incorporation model, however, is that it concentrates upon characterising general trends rather than on isolating factors that account for differences in the process of incorporation. Linked to this is the lack of attention to how particular social categories deal with externalisation, scientification and centralisation. For example, only in recent writings does Benvenuti acknowledge the importance of viewing contrasting patterns of incorporation as 'negotiated orders' that emerge as a result of the material and symbolic changes that take place between the various participants, including those representing the state (Benvenuti and Mommaas 1985).

These remarks provide a natural bridge to the third perspective, which adopts an actor-oriented approach to problems of agrarian development and State intervention. The issues here can be summarised quite simply by stating that an actor perspective aims to bring out the significance of building into the analysis some account of 'human agency'. This, as I suggested earlier, entails both the idea of individuals or groups developing social strategies (on the basis of existing knowledge, resources and capabilities) and that of emergent organisational forms that may acquire their own dynamics and thus shape future choice. Applying this theoretical perspective to agrarian problems and to questions of the State and policy leads one to a fuller appreciation of the complexities of intervention processes. It emphasises the theoretical importance of considering differential responses and outcomes to intervention, and thus exposes the limitations of highly generalised models. It criticises simple planning models that assume a three-step process of policy, implementation and outcomes, and points to the need to examine how policy is transformed during the process of implementation. It posits that State policy is not only determined by major structural factors (e.g. international markets, the state of capital accumulation on a global and national scale, and the influence of class struggle), but also by the social interests, ideologies and administrative styles of the State's political and bureaucratic elite. It also stresses the value of undertaking comparative studies of the social impact of particular forms of State intervention at the regional and local levels.

The underlying concept of the State in such models is difficult to capture succinctly, but a pluralist view predominates. The State consists of multiple interests and organisations that are involved in a series of struggles over resources, policies, ideologies, and the control of particular institutional domains. The strategies developed by the different actors, and how successful they are, are of course influenced by relationships, constituencies and resources outside the area of State power. The latter include not only the so-called dominant class or classes but also those that are regarded as relatively weak economically and politically at national level. The latter may have a significant influence on the outcomes of particular State interventions at local or regional level, and sometimes there are repercussions on State policy or on the standing and personnel of particular government institutions.

Actor-oriented studies therefore concentrate upon analysing the struggles that occur between these different economic and political actors. In the foregoing review, I argued the case for more systematic work on the types of 'interface' that develop between local groups (in this instance, farmers and other rural inhabitants) and intervening parties, and provided a brief discussion of some of the key dimensions for developing such a research strategy. I also suggested that it was important to situate interface analysis within a broad structural framework in order to explore the ways in which the benefits and penalties of development policy and intervention are distributed among different social sectors. In this way it becomes possible to re-examine some of the critical issues raised in the other approaches, such as the degrees of capital subsumption, institutional incorporation and State centralisation affecting different agrarian classes. The bringing together of an actor and a structural perspective presents certain unresolved theoretical issues but is clearly important if we are to go beyond existing formulations on agrarian development and State intervention.

Bibliography

Abate, A. and Teklu, U. (1982), 'Land Reform and Peasant Associations in Ethiopa: A Case Study of Two Widely Differing Regions', in Bhaduri and Rahman (eds.), pp. 58–89.

Abdullah. T. and Zeidenstein, S. (1976), 'Finding Ways to Learn About Rural Women: Experiences From a Pilot Project in Bangladesh', Seminar on the Project of Women in Socio-Economic Development in Bangladesh, Dacca.

Adams, A. (1981), 'The Senegal River Valley', In Heyer *et al.* (eds.), pp. 325–53.

Adnan, S. R. *et al.* (1976), 'Social Change and Rural Women: Possibilities of Participation', paper presented at the Seminar on the Project of Women in Socio-Economic Development in Bangladesh, Dacca.

Agar, M. (1980), *The Professional Stranger: An Informal Introduction to Ethnography*, Academic Press, New York.

Ahooja-Patel, K. (1982), 'Another development with women', *Development Dialogue*, 1/2, pp. 17–28.

Alavi, H. (1973), 'Peasant classes and primordial loyalties', *Journal of Peasant Studies*, I, 1, pp. 26–62.

Alavi, H. and Shanin, T. (eds.) (1982), *Introduction to the Sociology of 'Developing Societies'*, Macmillan, London.

Almy, S. (1979), 'Anthropologists and development agencies', *American Anthropologist*, LXXIX, 2, pp. 280–92.

Amin, S. (1974), *Accumulation on a World Scale*, Monthly Review Press, New York.

Apthorpe, R. (1970), 'Development Studies and Social Planning', in Apthorpe (ed.), pp. 1–28.

Apthorope, R. (ed.) (1970), *People, Planning and Development*

Studies, Frank Cass, London.

Arce, A. (1986), *Agricultural Policy Administration in a Less Developed Country: The Case of SAM in Mexico*, PhD thesis, University of Manchester.

Arce, A. and Long, N. (1986), 'The Dynamics of Knowledge Interfaces Between Mexican Agricultural Bureaucrats and Peasants: A Case Study from Jalisco', paper presented to the EIDOS workshop, School of Oriental and African Studies, University of London.

Ayres, R. L. (1983), *Banking on the Poor*, MIT Press, Cambridge, Mass. and London.

Bagadion, B. and Korten, F. (1985), 'Developing Irrigators' Organisations: A Learning Process Approach', in Cernea (ed.), pp. 52–90.

Baran, P. (1957), *The Political Economy of Growth*, Monthly Review Press, New York.

Barnett, T. (1981), 'Evaluating the Gezira Scheme: Black Box or Pandora's Box?' in Heyer *et al.* (eds), pp. 306–24.

Bates, R. H. (1983), *Essays on the Political Economy of Rural Africa*, Cambridge University Press, Cambridge.

Batley, R. (1983), *Power Through Bureaucracy: Urban Political Analysis in Brazil*, Gower, Aldershot.

Bennett, J. (1981), *Of Time and Enterprise: North American Family Farm Management in the Context of Resource Marginality*, University of Minnesota Press, Minneapolis.

Benvenuti, B. (1975), 'General systems theory and entrepreneurial autonomy in farming: towards a new feudalism or towards democratic planning?', *Sociologia Ruralis*, XV, 1/2, pp. 47–62.

Benvenuti, B. and Mommaas, L. (1985), *De Technologisch Administratieve Taakomgeving van Landbouwbedrijven: een Onderzoeksprogramma op het Terrein van Economische Sociologie van de Landbouw*, Department of Sociology of Western Countries, Wageningen.

Berg, E. (1975), *The Recent Economic Evolution of the Sahel*, Center for Economic Research, University of Michigan, Ann Arbor, Michigan.

Berger, P. (1977), *Pyramids of Sacrifice*, Penguin, Harmondsworth.

Bernstein, H. (1977), 'Notes on capital and peasantry', *Review of African Political Economy*, 10, pp. 60–73.

Bernstein, H. (1981), 'Notes on state and peasantry in Tanzania', *Review of African Political Economy*, 21, pp. 44–62.

Bernstein, H. (1986), 'Is There a Concept of Petty Commodity Production Generic to Capitalism?', paper presented to the 13th

European Congress for Rural Sociology. Forthcoming revised version in special issue of *Social Analysis* (edited by A. MacEwan Scott) on 'Rethinking Petty Commodity Production'.

Bhaduri, A. and Rahman, M. (eds.) (1982), *Studies in Rural Participation*, Oxford University Press, New Delhi.

Boeke, J. (1953), *Economics and Economic Policy in Dual Societies*, Willnink, Haarlem.

Booth, D. (1985), 'Marxism and development sociology: interpreting the impasse', *World Development*, XIII, 7, pp. 761–87.

Boserup, E. (1970), *Woman's Role in Economic Development*, Allen & Unwin, London.

Box, L. (1984), 'Survey on Trial: Sociological Contributions to Adaptive Agricultural Research', paper presented to the World Congress of Rural Sociology, Manilla.

Bromley, R.(ed.) (1979), *The Urban Informal Sector*, Pergamon Press, Oxford.

Brown, L. D. (1983), *Managing Conflict at Organizational Interfaces*, Addison-Wesley, Reading, Mass.

Bulmer, M. *et al.* (1986), *Social Science and Social Policy*, Allen & Unwin, London.

Bulmer, M. and Warwick, D. (eds.) (1983), *Social Research in Developing Countries: Surveys and Censuses in the Third World*, John Wiley, Chichester.

Burawoy, M. (1985), *The Politics of Production: Factory Regimes Under Capitalism and Socialism*, Verso Press, New Left Books, London.

Burgess, R. (1979), 'Petty Commodity Housing or Dweller Control?', in Bromley (ed.), pp. 1105–33.

Burgess, R. (1982), *Field Research: a Source Book and Field Manual*, Allen & Unwin, London.

Burgess, R. (1984), *In the Field: an Introduction to Field Research*, Allen & Unwin, London.

Caballero, J. M. (1980), *Agricultura, reforma agraria y pobreza campesina*, Instituto de Estudio Peruanos, Lima.

Caplan, N. *et al.* (1975), *The Use of Social Science Knowledge in Policy Decisions at National Level*, Institute for Social Research, University of Michigan, Ann Arbor, Michigan.

Carley, M. (1981), *Social Measurement and Social Indicators*, Allen & Unwin, London.

Carley, M. (1986), 'Tools for policy-making: indicators and impact assessment', in Bulmer *et al.*, pp. 126–54.

Carlos, M. L. and Anderson, B. (1981), 'Political Brokerage and Network Politics in Mexico: The Case of the Dominance System', in Willer and Anderson (eds.)

Casley, D. and Lury, D. (1981), *Data Collection in Developing Countries*, Clarendon Press, Oxford.

Cernea, M. (1981), *Land Tenure Systems and Social Implications of Forestry Development Programs*, World Staff Bank Working Paper No. 452, Washington D.C.

Cernea, M. (1982), *Indigenous Anthropologists and Development-Oriented Research*, World Bank Reprint Series No. 208, Washington D.C.

Cernea, M. (1983), *A Social Methodology for Community Participation in Local Investments: The Experience of Mexico's PIDER Program*, World Bank Staff Working Paper No. 598, Washington D.C.

Cernea, M., (ed.) (1985), *Putting People First: Sociological Variables in Rural Development*, Oxford University Press/World Bank, New York and London.

Chambers, R. (1983), *Rural Development: Putting the Last First*, Longman, London.

Chambers, R. (1985), 'Shortcut methods of gathering social information for rural development projects', in Cernea (ed.), pp. 399–415.

Chenery, H. *et al.* (1974), *Redistribution With Growth*, Oxford University Press, London.

Chinappa, B. (1977), 'The North Arcot sample survey', in B. H. Farmer (ed.), pp. 37–44.

CIMMYT economics staff (1984), 'The Farming Systems Perspective and Farmer Participation in the Development of Appropriate Technology', in Eicher and Staatz (eds.), pp. 362–77.

Clammer, J. (ed.) (1978), *Towards a New Economic Anthropology*, Macmillan, London.

Clayton, E. (1983), *Agriculture, Poverty and Freedom in Developing Countries*, Macmillan, London.

Cleland, J. and Hobcraft, J. (eds.) (1985), *Reproductive Change in Developing Countries: Insights from the World Fertility Survey*, Oxford University Press, London.

Cochrane, G. (1976), 'The Perils of Unconventional Anthropology', in Pitt (ed.), pp. 57–69.

Colson, E. (1960), *The Social Organisation of the Gwembe Tonga*, Manchester University Press, Manchester.

Conlin, S. (1985), 'Anthropological Advice in a Government Context', in Grillo and Rew (eds.), pp. 73–87.

Coppock, J. T. and Sewell, W. R. D. (eds.) (1976), *Spatial Dimensions of Public Policy*, Pergamon, Oxford.

Cosio, A. (1981), 'Community Development in Mexico', in Dore and Mars (eds.), pp. 337–432.

Coulson, A. (1981), 'Agricultural Policies in Mainland Tanzania, 1946–76', in Heyer *et al.*, pp. 52–89.

Coward, E. W. (1985), 'Technical and social change in currently irrigated regions: rules, roles and rehabilitation', in Cernea (ed.), pp. 27–51.

Dahl, R. (1961), *Who Governs? Democracy and Power in the American City*, Yale University Press, New Haven.

Derman, W. and Whiteford, S. (eds.) (1985), *Social Impact Analysis and Development Planning in the Third World*, Westview Press, Boulder, Colorado.

Development Dialogue (1982), 'Another Development with Women', 1–2, Dag Hammarskjold Foundation, Motal, Sweden.

Dore, R. (1976), *The Diploma Disease*, Allen & Unwin, London.

Dore, R. and Mars, Z. (eds.) (1981), *Community Development*, Croom Helm, London.

Dulansey, M. (1977), *Discussion on Women in Development*, CARE.

Dyson, T. and Crook, N. (eds.) (1984), *India's Demography: Essays on the Contemporary Population*, South Asia Publishers, New Delhi.

Eicher, C. and Staatz, J. (eds.) (1984), *Agricultural Development in the Third World*, Johns Hopkins University Press, London.

Elliot, C. *et al.* (1982), *Real Aid: A Strategy for Britain*, The Independent Group on British Aid, Oxford.

FAO (1979), *Participation of the Poor in Rural Organisations*, Rome.

Farmer, B. H. (ed.) (1977), *Green Revolution? Technology and Change in Rice-Growing Areas of Tamil Nadu and Sri Lanka*, Macmillan, London.

Foster, G. M. *et al.* (eds.) (1979), *Long-Term Field Research in Social Anthropology*, Academic Press, New York.

Frank, A. G. (1967), *Capitalism and Underdevelopment in Latin America*, Monthly Review Press, New York.

Frank, A. G. (1969), *Latin America: Underdevelopment or Revolution*, Monthly Review Press, New York.

Frank, A. G. (1971), *The Sociology of Development and the Underdevelopment of Sociology*, Pluto, London.

Freire, P. (1972), *Pedagogy of the Oppressed*, Penguin, Harmonds-worth.

Gaikwad, V. (1981), 'Community Development in India', in Dore and Mars (eds.), pp. 245–334.

Gale, D., Johnson, G. and Smith, G. E. (eds.) (1983), *The Role of Markets in the World Food Economy*, Westview Press, Boulder, Colorado.

Galjart, B. (1981), 'Counterdevelopment', *Community Development Journal*, XVI, pp. 88–96.

de Garine, I. (1978), 'Population, production and culture in the plains societies of Northern Cameroon and Chad: the anthropologist in development projects', *Current Anthropology*, XIX, 1, pp. 42–65.

Geertz, C. (1963), *Peddlers and Princes: Social Change in Economic Modernization in Two Indonesian Towns*, University of Chicago Press. Chicago.

Geschiere, P. (1984), 'Segmentary societies and the authority of the State: problems of implementing rural development in the Maka villages in south-eastern Cameroon', *Sociologia Ruralis*, XXIV, 1, pp. 10–29.

Giddens, A. (1979), *Central Problems in Social Theory: Action, Structure and Contradiction in Social Analysis*, Macmillan, London.

Glvanis, K. R. G. (1984), *Non-Capitalist Relations and the Small Peasant Household in Rural Egypt*, PhD thesis, University of Hull.

Gow, D. and VanSant, J. (1983), 'Beyond the rhetoric of rural development participation: how can it be done?', *World Development*, XI, pp. 427–46.

Gran, G. (1983), *Development By People*, Praeger, New York.

Gray, J. (1982), 'China's new agricultural revolution', *IDS Bulletin*, XIII, 4, pp. 36–43.

Gray, J. (1984), 'The state and the rural economy in the People's Republic of China', *IDS Bulletin*, XV, 2, pp. 11–17.

Greenfield, S. M. *et al.* (eds.) (1979), *Entrepreneurs in Cultural Context*, University of New Mexico Press, Albuquerque.

Griffin, K. (1974), *The Political Economy of Agrarian Change*, Macmillan, London.

Grillo, R. and Rew, A. (eds.) (1985), *Social Anthropology and Development Policy*, Tavistock, London and New York.

Grindle, M. (1977), *Bureaucrats, Peasants and Politicians in Mexico: A Case Study in Policy*, University of California Press, Berkeley and Los Angeles.

Grindle, M. (ed.) (1980), *Politics and Policy Implementation in the Third World*, Princeton University Press, Princeton, New Jersey.

Grindle, M. (1985), *State and Countryside: Development Policy and Agrarian Politics in Latin America*, Johns Hopkins University Press, Baltimore and London.

Hagen, E. (1962), *On the Theory of Social Change*, Dorsey Press, Homewood.

Hall, A. (1978), *Drought and Irrigation in North-East Brazil*, Cambridge University Press, Cambridge.

Hall, A. (1986), 'Community Participation and Rural Development', in Midgley *et al.*, pp. 87–104.

Hamilton, N. (1982), *The Limits of State Autonomy: Post-Revolutionary Mexico*, Princeton University Press, Princeton.

Haque, W. *et al.* (1977), 'Towards a theory of rural development', *Development Dialogue*, II, pp. 1–22.

Hardiman, M. (1970), 'A preliminary study of the role of women in some Akan rural communities', *Legon Family Research Papers*, No. 1, pp. 102–28, Institute of African Studies, Ghana.

Hardiman, M. (1974), 'Women in Maiduguri: Some Aspects of Their Lives', in Max Lock Group.

Hardiman, M. (1977), *Konkonuru: a Study of a Ghanaian Village*, mimeo., London School of Economics, London.

Hardiman M. (1984a), 'Social Surveys and Social Planning', in Midgley and Piachaud (eds.), pp. 56–86.

Hardiman, M. (1984b), 'Some lessons to be learnt from small-scale community health projects in India', in Dyson and Crook (eds.), pp. 127–40.

Hardiman, M. (1986), 'People's Involvement in Health and Medical Care', in Midgley *et al.*, pp. 45–69.

Hardiman, M. and Midgley, J. (1978), 'Foreign consultants in development planning: the need for an alternative approach', *Journal of Administration Overseas*, XVII, 4, pp. 232–44.

Hardiman, M. and Midgley, J. (1980), 'Training social planners for social development', in *International Social Work*, XXIII, 3, pp. 2–15.

Hardiman, M. and Midgley, J. (1982), *The Social Dimensions of Development*, Wiley, Chichester.

Hardjono, J. (1983), 'Rural development in Indonesia: the 'top-down' approach', in Lea and Chaudhri (eds.), pp. 38–65.

Harrell-Bond, B. E. (1986), *Imposing Aid: Emergency Assistance to*

Refugees, Oxford University Press, Oxford.

Harriss, J. (ed.) (1982), *Rural Development: Theories of Peasant Economy and Agrarian Change*, Hutchinson, London.

Hayek, F. (1944), *The Road to Serfdom*, Routledge & Kegan Paul, London.

Heyer, J. *et al.* (eds.) (1981), *Rural Development in Tropical Africa*, Macmillan, London.

Higgins, P. (1956), 'The dualistic theory of underdeveloped areas', *Economic Development and Cultural Change*, IV, pp. 99–115.

Hilhorst, J. G. M. and Klatter, M. (eds.) (1985), *Social Development in the Third World: Levels of Living Indicators and Social Planning*, Croom Helm, London.

Hill, P. (1957), *The Gold Coast Cocoa Farmers*, Oxford University Press, London.

Hill, P. (1963), *The Migrant Cocoa Farmers of South Ghana*, Cambridge University Press, Cambridge.

Hill, P. (1986) *Development Economics on Trial: the Anthropological Case for a Prosecution*, Cambridge University Press, Cambridge.

Hoogvelt A. (1982), *The Third World in Global Development*, Macmillan, London.

Horesh, E. (1981), 'Academics and experts or the death of the high-level technical assistant', *Development and Change*, XII, pp. 611–18.

Hoselitz, B. F. (1960), *Sociological Factors in Economic Development*, Free Press, New York.

Howery, C. (1984), 'Sociologist aids agricultural projects in Caribbean', *Footnotes*, XII, 2, p. 7.

Husain, T. (1976), 'Use of Anthropologists in Project Appraisal by the World Bank', in Pitt (ed.), pp. 71–81.

Hyden, G. (1980), *Beyond Ujamaa in Tanzania: Underdevelopment and an Uncaptured Peasantry*, Heinemann, London.

IDB, Inter-American Development Bank (1984), *Listas de Comprobacion Socio-Culturales*, mimeo., Washington, D.C.

IFAD, International Fund for Agricultural Development (1983), *The Role of Rural Credit Projects in Reaching the Poor*, Rome.

Jain, D. (1980), *Women's Quest for Power: Five Indian Case Studies*, Vikas, Ghaziabad.

Janowitz, M. (1970), 'Sociological models and social policy', in Janowitz, pp. 243–59.

Janowitz, M. (1970), *Political Conflict*, Quadrangle Books, Chicago.

Janowitz, M. (1971), *Sociological Models and Social Policy*, General Learning Press, Morristown.

de Janvry, A. (1981), *The Agrarian Question and Reformism in Latin America*, Johns Hopkins University Press, Baltimore and London.

de Janvry, A. (1983), 'Why do governments do what they want to do? The case of food price policy', in Gale, Johnson and Smith (eds.)

de Kadt, E. (1974), 'Introduction' in de Kadt and Williams (eds.), pp. 1–19.

de Kadt. E. (1982), 'Community participation for health', *World Development*, X, pp. 573–84.

de Kadt, E. and Williams, G. (eds.) (1974), *Sociology and Development*, Tavistock, London.

Kearl, B. (ed.) (1976), *Field Data Collection in the Social Sciences: Experiences in Africa and the Middle East*, Agricultural Development Council Inc., New York.

Kottak, C. (1985), 'When People Don't Come First: Some Sociological Lessons from Completed Projects', in Cernea (ed.) (1985), pp. 323–58.

Krantz, L. (1980), *Anthropology in Development Co-operation: A Swedish Model*, Department of Social Anthropology, University of Stockholm.

Lea, D. A. and Chaudhri, D. P. (eds.) (1983), *Rural Development and the State*, Methuen, London.

Leeds, A. (1964), 'Brazilian careers and social structure: a case history and model', *American Anthropologist*, LXVI, pp. 1321–47.

Lewis, W. A. (1954), 'Economic development with unlimited supplies of labour', *The Manchester School*, XXII, pp. 139–99.

Lewis, W. A. (1955), *The Theory of Economic Growth*, Allen & Unwin, London.

Lindblom, C. (1980), *The Policy-Making Process*, Prentice-Hall, Englewood Cliffs, New Jersey.

Lipsky, M. (1980), *Street Level Bureaucracy: Dilemmas of the Individual in Public Services*, Russell Sage Foundation, New York.

Lissner, J. (1977), *The Politics of Altruism*, Lutheran World Federation, Geneva.

Lloyd, P. (1979), *Slums of Hope?*, Penguin, Harmondsworth.

Long, N. (1968), *Social Change and the Individual: Social and Religious Responses to Innovation in a Zambian Rural Community*, Manchester University Press, Manchester.

Long, N. (1977), *An Introduction to the Sociology of Rural Develop-*

ment, Tavistock, London.

Long, N. (1979), 'Multiple Enterprise in the Central Highlands of Peru', in Greenfield *et al.* (eds.).

Long, N. (1984), 'Creating Space for Change: A Perspective on the Sociology of Development', Inaugural Lecture, Agricultural University, Wageningen.

Long, N. and Richardson, P. (1978), 'Informal Sector, Petty Commodity Production and Social Relations of Small-Scale Enterprise', in Clammer (ed.).

Long, N. and Roberts, B. (1984), *Miners, Peasants and Entrepreneurs: Regional Development in the Central Highlands of Peru*, Cambridge University Press, Cambridge.

Long, N. *et al.* (1986), 'The Commoditization Debate: Labour Process, Strategy and Social Network', Papers of the Department of Sociology, Agricultural University, Wageningen.

Mabogunje, A. L. (1976), 'The Population Census of Nigeria, 1973', in Coppock and Sewell (eds.), pp. 207–26.

Mair, L. (1984), *Anthropology and Development*, Macmillan, London.

Martinez, S. T. (1983), *Los Campesinos y el Estado en Mejico*, PhD thesis, Universidad Iberoamericana, Mexico.

Max Lock Group (1974), *The Survey and Planning of Maiduguri*, Maiduguri.

Mazumdar, V. (1982), 'Another development with women: a view from Asia', *Development Dialogue*, 1/2, pp. 65–73.

Mbilinyi, M. (1975), 'Tanzanian women confront the past and the future', *Futures*, October.

Melotti, U. (1977), *Marx and the Third World*, Macmillan, London.

Midgley, J. (1984a), 'Fields of Practice and Professional Roles for Social Planners', in Midgley and Piachaud (eds.), pp. 11–33.

Midgley, J. (1984b), 'Social welfare implications of development paradigms', *Social Service Review*, LVIII, pp. 181–9.

Midgley, J. and Piachaud, D. (1984), 'Social Indicators and Social Planning', in Midgley and Piachaud (eds.), pp. 34–55.

Midgley, J. and Piachaud, D. (eds.), (1984), *The Fields and Methods of Social Planning*, Heinemann Educational Books, London.

Midgley, J. *et al.* (1986), *Community Participation, Social Development and the State*, Methuen, London.

Miles, I. (1985), *Social Indicators for Human Development*, Frances Pinter, London.

Miliband, R. (1969), *The State in Capitalist Society*, Basic Books, New

York.

Morgenstern, O. (1963), *On The Accuracy of Economics*, Princeton University Press, Princeton.

Morris, M. D. (1979), *Measuring the Conditions of the World's Poor: the Physical Quality of Life Index*, Pergamon, Oxford.

Mukhopadhyay, M. (1984), *Silver Shackles: Women and Development in India*, Oxfam, Oxford.

Muntemba, M. (1982), 'Women as food producers and suppliers in the twentieth century: the case of Zambia', *Development Dialogue*, 1/2, pp. 29–50.

Murthy, M. N. (1978), 'Use of sample surveys in national planning in developing countries', in Namboodiri (ed.), pp. 231–53.

Murthy, M. N. and Roy, A. S. (1983), 'Development of the sample design of the Indian National Sample Survey during its first 25 rounds', in Bulmer and Warwick (eds.), pp. 109–23.

Mushi, S. (1981), 'Community Development in Tanzania', in Dore and Mars (eds.), pp. 139–242.

Myrdal, G. (1962), *Value in Social Theory*, Routledge & Kegan Paul, London.

Myrdal, G. (1968), *Asian Drama: An Inquiry Into the Poverty of Nations*, Penguin, Harmondsworth.

Mydral, G. (1970), *The Challenge of World Poverty*, Penguin, Harmondsworth.

Namboodiri, N. K. (ed.) (1978), *Survey Sampling and Measurement*, Academic Press, New York.

Norman, D. (1978), *The Farming Systems Approach: Relevancy for the Small Farmer*, mimeo., Michigan State University, Ann Abor.

Oakley, P. and Marsden, D. (1984), *Approaches to Participation in Rural Development*, International Labour Office, Geneva.

Oakley, P. and Winder, D. (1981), *The Concept and Practice of Rural Social Development*, Manchester Papers on Development, Studies in Rural Development, University of Manchester.

O'Barr, W. M. *et al.* (eds.) (1973), *Survey Research in Africa: its Applications and Limits*, Northwestern University Press, Evanston, Illinois.

ODA, Overseas Development Administration (1982), *Policy Guidance Note on the Role of Social Development Advisers*, PGN No. 26, London.

ODA (1983), *The Lessons of Experience: Evaluation Work in ODA*, London.

O'Donnell, G. (1978), 'Reflections on the patterns of change in the bureaucratic–authoritarian state', *Latin American Research Review*, XIII, 1, pp. 3–38.

OECD (1978), *Multi-Purpose Household Surveys in Developing Countries*, Development Centre of the OECD, Paris.

Oppong, C. (1976), 'Ghanaian Women Teachers and Workers, Kin, Wives and Mothers: A Study of Conjugal Family Solidarity – Norms, Reality and Stress', paper presented at the *Conference on Women and Development*, Wellesley, Mass., June 2–6.

Ortiz, S. (1973), *Uncertainties in Peasant Farming: A Colombian Case*, Athlone Press, London.

Oxfam (1985), *The Field Directors' Handbook: An Oxfam Manual for Development Workers*, 4th, edn., Oxford University Press, Oxford.

Padua, J. and Vanneph, A. (eds.) (1986), *Poder Local, Poder Regional*, El Colegio de Mejico/CEMCA, Mexico City.

Palmer, I. (1977), 'Rural women and the basic needs approach to development', *International Labour Review*, 115.1.

Panse, V. G. (1958), 'Some comments on the objectives and methods of the 1960 World Census of Agriculture', *Bulletin of the International Statistical Institute*, 36, pp. 22–7

Payer, C. (1982), *The World Bank: A Critical Analysis*, Monthly Review Press, London.

Pearse, A. (1975), *The Latin American Peasant*, Frank Cass, London.

Pearse, A. (1980), *Seeds of Plenty, Seeds of Want*, Clarendon Press, Oxford.

Pearse, A. and Stiefel, M. (1981), *Debaters' Comments on 'Inquiry into Participation: A Research Approach'*, United Nations Research Institute for Social Development, Geneva.

Peil, M. *et al.* (1982), *Social Science Research Methods: An African Handbook*, Hodder & Stoughton, London.

de la Pena, G. (1986), 'Poder Local, Poder Regional: Perspectivas Socioantropológicas', in Padua and Vanneph (eds.).

Perret, H. *et al.* (1980), *Human Factors in Project Work*, World Bank Staff Working Paper No. 397, Washington D.C.

Pitt, D. C. (ed.) (1976), *Development From Below: Anthropologists and Development Situations*, Mouton, The Hague.

van der Ploeg, J. D. (1986), 'The Agricultural Labour Process and Commoditization', in Long *et al.*

van der Ploeg, J. D. and Bolhuis, E. E. (1985), *Boerenarbeid en Stijlen van Landbouwbeoefening*, PhD thesis, University of Leiden.

Pollnac, R. (1981), *Sociocultural Aspects of Developing Small-Scale Fisheries: Delivering Services to the Poor*, World Bank Staff Working Paper No. 490, Washington D.C.

Poulantzas, N. (1973), *Political Power and Social Classes*, New Left Books, London.

Price, D. (1985), 'The World Bank vs native peoples: a consultant's view', *The Ecologist*, XV, 1/2, pp. 73–7.

Rihani, M. (1978), *Development as if Women Mattered: An Annotated Bibliography with a Third World Focus*, Occasional Paper No. 10, Overseas Development Council, Washington, D.C.

Rimmer, D. (1982), 'Official statistics', in Peil *et al.*, pp. 47–58.

Robertson, A. (1984), *People and the State: An Anthropology of Planned Development*, Cambridge University Press, Cambridge.

Rogers, B. (1980), *The Domestication of Women: Discrimination in Developing Societies*, Tavistock, London.

Rondinelli, D. (1983), *Development Projects as Policy Experiments*, Methuen, London.

Rosenstein-Rodan, P. (1943), 'Problems of industrialisation in southern and eastern Europe', *Economic Journal*, LIII, pp. 205–11.

Rostow, W. (1960), *The Stages of Economic Growth: A Non-Communist Manifesto*, Cambridge University Press, Cambridge.

Sanderson, S. E. (1986), *The Transformation of Mexican Agriculture: International Structure and the Politics of Rural Change*, Princeton University Press, Princeton.

Scott, J. C. (1985), *Weapons of the Weak: Everyday Forms of Peasant Resistance*, Yale University Press, New Haven, Connecticut.

Scudder, T. (1962), *The Ecology of the Gwembe Tribe*, Manchester University Press, Manchester.

Scudder, T. and Colson, E. (1979), 'Long-term research in the Gwembe Valley, Zambia', in Foster *et al.* (eds.), pp. 227–54.

Seers, D. (1972), 'The Meaning of Development', in Uphoff and Ilchman (eds.), pp. 123–9.

Shepherd, G. (1984), *Responding to the Cooperative Needs of Rural People. A Report to Oxfam on Kenya*, Oxford.

de Silva, G. *et al.* (1982), 'Bhoomi Sena: A Land Army in India', in Bhaduri and Rahman (eds.), pp. 151–69.

Skocpol, T. (1979), *States and Social Revolution: A Comparative Analysis of France, Russia and China*, Cambridge University Press, Cambridge.

Spittler, G. (1983), 'Administration in a peasant state', *Sociologia Ruralis*, XXIII, 2, pp. 130–44.

Srinivas, M. N. *et al.* (1979), *The Fieldworker and the Field: Problems and Challenges in Sociological Investigation*, Oxford University Press, Delhi.

Stavenhagen, R. (1971), 'Decolonising applied social science', *Human Organization*, XXX, 4, pp. 333–57.

Steady, F. (1982), 'African women, industrialization and another development: a global perspective', *Development Dialogue*, 1/2, pp. 51–64.

Steifel, L. *et al.* (eds.) (1982), *Social Sciences and Public Policy in the Developing World*, Lexington Books, Lexington, Mass.

Streeten, P. *et al.* (1981), *First Things First: Meeting Basic Needs in Developing Countries*, Oxford University Press, Oxford and New York.

Tobisson, E. (1986), Personal communication from the Development Study Unit, Department of Social Anthropology, University of Stockholm, 27 March.

United Nations (1951), *Measures for the Economic Development of the Underdeveloped Countries*, New York.

UNRISD, United Nations Research Institute for Social Development (1975), *Rural Cooperatives as Agents for Change*, Geneva.

Uphoff, N. (1985), 'Fitting Projects to People', in Cernea (ed.), pp. 359–95.

Uphoff, N. and Ilchman, W. (eds.) (1972), *The Political Economy of Development*, University of California Press, Berkeley.

USAID, United States Agency for International Development (1982), *AID Handbook 3, Appendix 3*, Washington D.C.

Ward, M. (1983), 'Missing the Point: Sampling Methods and Types of Error in Third World Surveys in Identifying Poverty Issues', in Bulmer and Warwick (eds.), pp. 125–42.

Warren, B. (1980), *Imperialism: Pioneer of Capitalism*, Verso, London.

Warwick, D. (1982), *Bitter Pills: Population Policies and Their Implementation in Eight Developing Countries*, Cambridge University Press, Cambridge.

Warwick, D. (1983), 'The K.A.P. Survey: dictates of mission v. demands of science', in Bulmer and Warwick (eds.), pp. 349–63.

Warwick, D. and Lininger, C. (1975), *The Sample Survey: Theory and Practice*, McGraw Hill, New York.

Waterston, A. (1965), *Development Planning: Lessons From Experience*, Johns Hopkins University Press, Baltimore and London.

Weiss, C. (1980), *Social Science and Decision-Making*, Columbia University Press, New York.

Wenger, G. (ed.) (1987), *The Research Relationship*, Allen & Unwin, London.

Willer, D. and Anderson, B. (eds.) (1981), *Networks, Exchange and Coercion*, Elsevier, New York and London.

Winder, D. (1979), *An Analysis of the Consequences of Government Attempts to Promote Community Development Through the Creation of Cooperative Institutions, With special reference to Rural Mexico*, PhD thesis, University of Manchester.

Winkler, J. (1976), 'Corporatism', *European Journal of Sociology*, XVII, pp. 100–36.

World Bank (1979), *Recognizing the 'Invisible' Women in Development: The World Bank's Experience*, Washington D.C.

World Bank (1982), 'Sociologists: putting people first in projects', *Report*, March-April, p. 5.

World Bank (1984), *Environmental Policies and Procedures*, Washington D.C.

Young, K. and Smith, S. (1982), 'Women's disadvantage: capitalist development and socialist alternatives in Britain', *Development Dialogue*, 1/2, pp. 85–100.

Zarkovitch, S. (1975), *Statistical Development*, Cairo University Press, Cairo.

About the authors

Anthony Hall is a Lecturer in Social Planning in Developing Countries at the London School of Economics. Major publications include *Drought and Irrigation in North-East Brazil* (1978); with J. Midgley and others, *Community Participation, Social Development and the State* (1986); and *Social Conflict in Brazilian Amazonia: the Grande Carajás Programme* (forthcoming).

James Midgley, formerly of the London School of Economics, is now Professor and Dean of the School of Social Work at Louisiana State University, Baton Rouge. He is co-author or editor of *The Social Dimensions of Development* (1982), *The Fields and Methods of Social Planning* (1984) and *Community Participation, Social Development and the State* (1986). His other major publications are *Professional Imperialism: Social Work in the Third World* (1981) and *Social Security, Inequality and the Third World* (1984).

Martin Bulmer is Senior Lecturer in Social Administration at the London School of Economics. He is author or editor of some fifteen books, including *Sociological Research Methods* (1977), *Mining and Social Change* (1978), The Uses of Social Research (1982), *Social Research in Developing Countries* (1983), *The Chicago School of Sociology (1984) and Social Science and Social Policy* (1986).

Margaret Hardiman taught in the Department of Social Administration at the London School of Economics from 1965 until 1986, where she was Convenor of the courses in Social Planning in Developing Countries; from 1968 to 1971 she was head of Social Administration at the University of Ghana. At present she teaches part time at the LSE and the Royal Institute of International Affairs. She is co-author of *The Social Dimensions of Development* (1982).

Norman Long is Professor of Sociology at the Agricultural University of Wageningen in the Netherlands. His major publications include *Social Change and the Individual: A Study of the Social and Religious Responses to Innovation* (1968), *An Introduction to the Sociology of Rural Development* (1977) and, with B. Roberts, *Miners, Peasants and Entrepreneurs: Regional Development in the Central Highlands of Peru* (1984).

Index